Decades ago, I was i
chapter of Proverbs
(thirty-one chapters for thirty-one days). I was recently astonished
to realize that because of that discipline, I've read the entire book
of Proverbs almost five hundred times. Yet in *Growing Kingdom
Wisdom*, Tom Yeakley points out several key insights from the
endless treasures of Proverbs that I had read but not recognized.
I believe that any Christian, but especially those in leadership roles,
could profit from the years of study that Yeakley has condensed in
this book. If you long to grow in Kingdom wisdom, along with
reading the Proverbs themselves, read this book.

> **DONALD S. WHITNEY,** professor of biblical spirituality and associate dean at
> The Southern Baptist Theological Seminary; author of *Spiritual Disciplines for the
> Christian Life* and *Praying the Bible*

Growing Kingdom Wisdom by Tom Yeakley is comprehensive,
challenging, and convicting. I count this as an essential study for
any leader who seeks an intentional path to godly wisdom and
spiritual growth. Yeakley generously provides tools that create the
discipline required for the divine process of transformation to
advance its work in you.

> **TAMI HEIM,** president and CEO, Christian Leadership Alliance

Wisdom is one of the qualities most needed by leaders, yet is
the hardest to develop. It is more of an art than a science, taking
time and humility to develop. Tom Yeakley has done a superb job
helping us know not only what Kingdom wisdom is but more
importantly, how to grow in it, letting its benefits impact every
area of our lives and leadership.

> **TOM HUGHES,** colead pastor, Christian Assembly Church; author of *Curious*
> and *Down to Earth*

The list of desirable leadership qualities fills thousands of books. Tom Yeakley condenses the list to one absolutely necessary element—*wisdom*. "Wisdom is supreme; therefore get wisdom. Though it cost all you have, get understanding" (Proverbs 4:7, NIV). Wisdom is the glue to all the other leadership qualities. The quest for godly wisdom seems to be too indefinable to be pursued. Tom beautifully takes the mystery out of the search and gives incredibly practical help in growing this life of wisdom. It's not a formula, but rather a process of practice, discovery, and deep commitment. The teaching of this book will give power to your life and leadership.

   JERRY E. WHITE, major general, United States Air Force (retired)

Wisdom is one of those blessings from God I honestly never thought of as something to be worked on. Received, yes of course, as Solomon received wisdom from the Lord. Earned by the wrinkles and gray hair of old age? Also of course. But something to actively and intentionally work toward? To be honest, no, I hadn't given that much thought. And yet Tom Yeakley has outlined a way to do just that in his book *Growing Kingdom Wisdom*. It made me pause, reflect, and pull out my yellow highlighter more than a few times!

   ROY GOBLE, author of *Salvaged*

GROWING

The Essential Qualities of a

KINGDOM

Mature Christian Leader

WISDOM

TOM YEAKLEY

A NavPress resource published in alliance
with Tyndale House Publishers, Inc.

NavPress is the publishing ministry of The Navigators, an international Christian organization and leader in personal spiritual development. NavPress is committed to helping people grow spiritually and enjoy lives of meaning and hope through personal and group resources that are biblically rooted, culturally relevant, and highly practical.

For more information, visit www.NavPress.com.

The Team:
Don Pape, Publisher
David Zimmerman, Acquisitions Editor
Elizabeth Schroll, Copy Editor
Julie Chen, Designer

Some of the anecdotal illustrations in this book are true to life and are included with the permission of the persons involved. All other illustrations are composites of real situations, and any resemblance to people living or dead is purely coincidental.

For information about special discounts for bulk purchases, please contact Tyndale House Publishers at csresponse@tyndale.com, or call 1-800-323-9400.

Cataloging-in-Publication Data is available.

ISBN 978-1-63146-916-9

Printed in the United States of America

25	24	23	22	21	20	19
7	6	5	4	3	2	1

To Dana, our three children, their spouses, our grandchildren,

and those I have had the privilege to lead and influence,

who continue to be patient with me in my pursuit of wisdom.

CONTENTS

FOREWORD

Wisdom is timeless, not trendy. While people of different generations have sought or ignored it, it has never wavered as the driver of lasting success and effective leadership, nor will it ever be supplanted by new inventions or technology.

Investing your time in reading this book is a wonderful way to start or improve your journey to wisdom.

Much is written about wisdom from the secular viewpoint, and certainly there are wonderful concepts and ideas to be learned in that writing. But wisdom ultimately comes from God. Knowing the source of true wisdom is essential to developing it in your own life, and this book illustrates that clearly.

I constantly remind myself of the story in 2 Chronicles 1 when God appeared to Solomon and said He'd give him whatever he asked.

Solomon could have understandably asked for wealth, strength, and long life, but instead, he asked for wisdom so he could lead the people. God's response? He gave Solomon wisdom and riches, wealth and glory. This is a classic example of putting first things first and getting the other things as a result.

Would you have asked for wisdom? Would I? Here is a paradox: Only those with some wisdom would know to ask for it. Obviously,

God gives us wisdom, but we are not exempt from applying our own thinking in the quest for it.

Tom Yeakley has a heart for next-generation leaders, and this book is not only proof of that but a contribution to those leaders' development. I share this commitment and passion, and I pray that these concepts are embraced by all who read them, but especially by our future leaders.

As someone who has the privilege to address, teach, and develop leaders, I often share this concept: If you want to lead better and be better, use the FIT tools—frequency, intensity, and technique. How does that relate to wisdom? To be wiser:

1. Increase the *frequency* with which you pursue, study, and reflect on wisdom. Replace lower-value activities with the more frequent intentional pursuit of wisdom.
2. Don't dally—use *intensity*. Be committed, devoted, and intensely focused on what you have experienced, what you have learned, and what you need to do to become wiser. Your growth in wisdom will be proportionate to the intensity with which you pursue it.
3. Use the best *techniques*. Rather than taking a haphazard approach (ironic if you are a student of wisdom), use the best systems and processes. Here's some great news: This book is full of techniques and processes for increasing wisdom.

The etymology of *philosophy* is "love of wisdom." By that standard, you are a philosopher in the most practical (and perhaps best) sense of the word for reading this book.

Mark Sanborn
Denver, Colorado

INTRODUCTION

If you don't know where you're going, you might not get there.
YOGI BERRA

Begin with the end in mind.
STEPHEN COVEY

I WAS SITTING across my desk from one of my direct reports. He had come to me for advice on how to solve a problem he was facing. His options were several—all with some good and bad consequences. Which one should he choose?

As I listened to him, I was having a conversation with myself. *He's going to expect me to have an answer for him. What should I tell him?* He had a good handle on the issue, but which of these solutions would be his best option? I wasn't sure what to do. It was a judgment call between a good, better, and seemingly best solution.

"I need wisdom, Lord," I prayed. "Give me wisdom that comes from You, Lord, to help me see what solution we should embrace here."

We often find ourselves out of our depth when seeking to solve problems or determine a way forward from our current situation. Issues that are black and white are quickly solved, but many problems are gray. They present with complexities we have never seen, and our options don't present as clear solutions.

The more responsibility one has, the more regularly one is dealing with these types of gray issues. The more obvious ones have been handled by others before they arrive at your desk.

Leaders in any context need wisdom, and Kingdom leaders desperately need it to lead well according to God's Kingdom values and purposes. This Kingdom we refer to is the rule and reign of Jesus Christ: Kingdom leaders are seeking to advance Christ's rule and reign among the people of this world.

Leaders in any context are reliant on wisdom, and the best leaders are conscious of that reliance and seek wisdom in every situation. In worldly contexts, Kingdom priorities are not necessarily valued, so solutions are based largely on judgment, which arises primarily from experience. For those who are observant, the repetition of experiences over time reveals patterns of actions and their resulting consequences. Thus, one can begin to predict certain outcomes based on decisions and choices made.

But without a fixed standard to know if something is truly wise, we are forced to measure our wisdom by results: If the results are what we desire, then we assume the pathway to achieving them was wise. This view of wisdom leads to "end justifies the means" thinking and ignores the higher moral values and eternal purposes of God's Kingdom.

Simply because one has a lot of experience does not necessarily mean that person is growing in wisdom. What is labeled *wisdom* could simply be repetition. Unintended consequences may be hidden from view; moral compromises may be clouded over. A leader's résumé may show significant growth, but perspective, insight, and discernment—true wisdom—may remain stagnant.

Those of us who accept the primacy of God's Kingdom have an objective standard—the Word of God—to test our decisions against.

Worldly wisdom can't claim such a standard, so the wisdom gained from experience is vulnerable to folly.

True wisdom is from God Himself. It is given to those who ask and pursue it from Him. It can come as a gift from God or be gained as one sorts experiences that align with Kingdom values and discards those that don't. We prioritize outcomes that further God's Kingdom purposes and bring honor and glory to Him. We seek to lead in ways that align with His Kingdom values as reflected in His character. *How* we arrive at our results is just as important as *what our results are.*

Several decades ago, I began to focus on the personal pursuit of wisdom, particularly as it applied to leadership. I was challenged by reading James 1:5: "If any of you lacks wisdom, let him ask God, who gives generously to all without reproach, and it will be given him." I had studied the life of Solomon and knew that his request for wisdom to lead was pleasing to the Lord. I knew, therefore, that I could ask for something similar and enter that same pursuit of wisdom with confidence that I, too, could find favor from the Lord and become a godly, wise Kingdom leader. But what is godly wisdom? How is it different from the wisdom of the world? How do we intentionally pursue it? Where do we begin? How do we know that we've obtained it? And how can we pass it along to someone else?

This book is my attempt to take the mystery out of pursuing wisdom. We'll look at what Kingdom wisdom is according to the Scriptures, breaking wisdom into its component parts and seeing how they interrelate. We'll contrast godly wisdom in its various attributes with the wisdom of the world to help us distinguish between the two. We will also address how wisdom applies to leadership as we seek to accomplish God's mission and the tasks He has called us to do.

Although this book is written with positional leaders in mind, *everyone* needs wisdom for living a life pleasing to God. All of us are striving for that end-of-life affirmation from the Lord: "Well done, good and faithful servant" (Matthew 25:23). If that is the goal, what road should we take now that will lead to that destination of becoming a wise leader in God's eyes? Whether you are just beginning a journey of pursuing God's wisdom or you desire a boost in your current wisdom-seeking journey, this book is for you.

When I talk to other people about their growth and development, we quickly move to two essentials of great leadership: character (a leader's personal example that backs up their words) and wisdom (a leader's quality of decision-making). This is true for all leaders regardless of context, but it is particularly true—and these qualities are particularly in view—for Kingdom leaders. They know that both their spiritual health and their Kingdom influence depend on their intentional pursuit of Christlike character and godly wisdom. But while a quick perusal of the leadership section of the local library or bookstore quickly validates "worldly wisdom," few leadership books ask how to know that God is pleased with our leadership. Asking that question is, in fact, counterintuitive to worldly wisdom. Leadership is too complex, the facts on the ground are shifting too quickly, and too many cultures are colliding in front of us to pause and reflect.

Yet a world that is so turbulent and chaotic demands a wisdom that is otherworldly. Kingdom leaders—those seeking to honor God with their leadership and accomplish His purposes—know that they must give an account of their leadership to the Lord (see Hebrews 13:17).

By God's help and grace, we can see character change and growth toward spiritual maturity over time. Yes, sometimes it seems like it's two steps forward and one backward, but overall, we can see net gains in our character development when we seek after it. We live and lead more out of who we are than what we know—especially when we are under pressure.

But good character alone does not ensure good leadership. There are many people with godly character who cannot lead! Competencies, strategies, and tactics must also be developed if one is to lead well. And underlying all of this must be the pursuit of the otherworldly wisdom of God's Kingdom. God-given wisdom brings God-honoring results that will stand the test of time.

GETTING THE MOST OUT OF THIS BOOK

This book is designed as a tool to help you become more intentional about pursuing godly wisdom—both for yourself and for those you are leading. The book addresses seven key aspects of godly wisdom and how to grow in these vital areas. A chapter is devoted to each of these seven components, describing how each can be identified and implemented.

It is not enough to simply *know* you must grow, however; you must also *become intentional* about growing. Therefore, the end of each chapter contains a short section to assist your reflection on the component of wisdom just discussed. Each devotional reflection consists of a few key Bible passages to study, items to incorporate into your prayer time, and suggested personal applications.

The appendix is an extension of these chapter resources. The wisdom-development resources in the appendix consist of four parts:

1. a topical Bible study;
2. Scripture-memory verses related to the topic;
3. personal prayer focus items; and
4. practical exercises for application in life and leadership.

Bible Study

The topical Bible studies in the chapters and the appendix are not meant to be exhaustive, only to get you started. Personal convictions are rooted in our lives by doing personal Bible study on a given issue. If you have placed your life under the authority of the Scriptures and desire to obey Him whom you serve, knowing what the Bible says on any subject is foundational. You must know the commands of God before you can obey them (see John 14:21).

Begin your pursuit of wisdom by doing the topical Bible study, developing and deepening your personal beliefs and convictions. Knowing what God says about wisdom and understanding its application to life and leadership will provide a great foundation for useful contribution. For more in-depth study on a topic, consider using a topical Bible to discover more related passages or cross-reference individual verses using a study Bible.

When you study the Bible, always be mindful that the desired outcome is to understand and apply the Word of God to your life. Follow the example of Ezra, who not only studied the Scriptures but also obeyed them and then taught them to others (see Ezra 7:10). D. L. Moody said, "The Bible was not given to increase our knowledge, but to change our lives."[1]

Memory Verses

Having developed and deepened your personal convictions, you can now begin to integrate them into your life. Memorizing selected passages (I've recommended some in the appendix) will provide you the opportunity to meditate on God's Word and give the Holy Spirit a tool He can use to shape and guide your decisions. He can bring these passages to your mind as you interact with people, make daily decisions, and solve problems.

You must train yourself to be sensitive to the prompting of His voice as you go through your daily responsibilities. The prophet Isaiah reminds us that we can count on the Lord's guidance: "Your ears shall hear a word behind you, saying, 'This is the way, walk in it'" (Isaiah 30:21).

Begin to memorize the suggested memory verses or select passages from the Bible study. Be sure to memorize the references along with the verses to enable you to recall them quickly and accurately. Many people find it helpful to repeat the reference before and after the verse as they memorize it.

To further develop the habit of Scripture memory, a helpful tool is the *Topical Memory System.*[2] Its sixty verses arranged in thirty discipleship topics will help lay a solid foundation in your heart and mind.

Prayer Items

The process of character transformation is a divine work that requires divine power for lasting change. Begin to pray regularly about these topics, asking God to help build them into your life. Ask God for sensitivity and a growing self-awareness of areas that require change. Pray for grace to grow and develop in these key aspects of wisdom.

Many people find it helpful to write out their prayer requests in a small notebook and pray through these prayer requests daily. A written guide can help bring focus and concentration as you pray. Consider taking an extended time away with the Lord—a half day, for example—to focus your prayer time on specific topics of concern or need. Ask the Lord to help you apply what you are learning.

Set aside regular time each day to pray over these areas of wisdom. The length of prayer time is not as important as the attitude of your heart. Earnestly asking God for help in character change, allowing the Spirit to speak to your heart, and then responding to His leading will create fertile ground for transformation. Seek to pray faithfully over these areas, remembering to thank God for positive changes you notice and confess your sins as He reveals them.

Practical Applications

Every component of wisdom has a suggested list of application exercises. Some exercises are short-term, with the objective of sensitizing you to areas for growth. Others are more long-term projects that require persistence and perseverance to see permanent change. It is not within your power to change—that is, to make yourself wise. These exercises simply present opportunities for the Lord to do a deeper, longer-lasting work within you. It is the Lord who changes you, not you yourself.

Paul reminds us to "walk in a manner worthy of the calling to which [we] have been called" (Ephesians 4:1), and we can do so by making sure that our practice matches our profession. Jesus had hard words for the religious leaders of His day whose knowledge and leadership practices were not congruent. God does not use hypocritical leaders for great Kingdom tasks! As James exhorts us, "Be doers of the word, and not hearers only, deceiving yourselves" (James 1:22).

The applications center on the tools most often used by God to shape us: the Word, prayer, and life experiences. Hopefully, as you apply what you learn, you will form new beliefs and behavior patterns that affect your life and leadership.

WISDOM IS A BLESSING

The pursuit of wisdom must be intentional for us to truly see it established in our lives. We are called to pursue wisdom as a priority. This endeavor will require effort, discipline, and a learner's heart, and it will be met with a blessing.

> Blessed is the one who finds wisdom,
>   and the one who gets understanding,
> for the gain from her is better than gain from silver
>   and her profit better than gold.
> She is more precious than jewels,
>   and nothing you desire can compare with her.
> Long life is in her right hand;
>   in her left hand are riches and honor.

Her ways are ways of pleasantness,
  and all her paths are peace.
She is a tree of life to those who lay hold of her;
  those who hold her fast are called blessed.

PROVERBS 3:13-18

You are about to begin a great journey of intentional personal growth and change. Set your face "like a flint" (Isaiah 50:7) to see it through. Don't be discouraged if it seems hard to measure change and growth; trust God to do what He has promised. "If any of you lacks wisdom, let him ask God . . . and it will be given him" (James 1:5). Trust Him who promises, "He who began a good work in you will bring it to completion at the day of Jesus Christ" (Philippians 1:6).

1

THE FOUNDATION OF
GODLY WISDOM

Everyone then who hears these words of mine and does them will be like a
wise man who built his house on the rock. And the rain fell, and the floods
came, and the winds blew and beat on that house, but it did not fall, because
it had been founded on the rock. And everyone who hears these words of
mine and does not do them will be like a foolish man who built his house
on the sand. And the rain fell, and the floods came, and the winds blew
and beat against that house, and it fell, and great was the fall of it.

JESUS, IN MATTHEW 7:24-27

BUILDING A HOUSE in the foothills of Colorado Springs, where I live, can be difficult. The soil near the mountains is a mixture of sand and clay. The clay component expands and contracts with the amount of moisture present, creating very unstable building sites. All builders must do soil tests before building begins and then design foundations that can adjust to the changing dynamics of the soil underneath. The soil type determines the foundation that is laid. And as with all buildings, it is the foundation that is the key to a solid, lasting structure.

To build a solid foundation for pursuing wisdom, we first must know the soil we are building on. The soil of our heart is where the foundation of wisdom is built.

Note what is said about Solomon in 1 Kings 10:24: "The whole earth sought the presence of Solomon to hear his wisdom, which God had put into his mind." And in Psalm 90:12 we read: "Teach us to number our days that we may get a heart of wisdom." It is within our hearts that wisdom resides, and it is the condition of our heart that determines whether godly wisdom is established.

So, we must examine our heart to know if we are ready for the construction of wisdom to begin.

Let's not assume that anyone can begin pursuing godly wisdom without first having the Holy Spirit residing within them. It is He who lays the foundation of the Word of God within us—giving us insight, leading us to truth and its application. Good heart soil for building is a heart that is submitted to the Lord Jesus in all areas of life and leadership. It is a heart that desires to please Him above all others and has decided to obey Him regardless of apparent cost. It is in this soil that a solid foundation for the building of wisdom can take place.

We follow the example of David, who said, "Prove me, O LORD, and try me; test my heart and my mind. For your steadfast love is before my eyes, and I walk in your faithfulness" (Psalm 26:2-3).

LEADERS WHO LACK GODLY WISDOM

Leaders who have not sought God's wisdom often rely on experience and intuition for guidance. Their decision-making is predicated on "Go with your gut." While there may be some benefit to this approach, it is limited to what a leader has learned, at a gut level, from prior relevant experiences, combined with the extent to which a leader has submitted themselves to the lordship of Christ. As much experience as we may amass, we are still always finite: We can see only so far, and we can make only so much sense of what we can see. Contrast that with God, who says of Himself: "As the heavens are higher than the earth, so are my ways higher than your ways and my thoughts than your thoughts" (Isaiah 55:9). God gives revelation to leaders who rely on His Spirit.

Leaders who lack godly wisdom may confuse accumulated knowledge and experience with true wisdom. God's leaders, however, understand the limitations of their knowledge and understanding. They confess their shortcomings and their need for godly insight and discernment. They acknowledge that His ways and thoughts are higher, and they ask the Lord for guidance and help. This attitude of humility and teachability moves them to dependent prayer. Better to go with God than to go with your gut!

Leaders who have not acknowledged the gap between what they can know and what God can reveal to them may assume that the patterns of the world are also the patterns of the Kingdom. Seeking to understand the complexities of leadership, they rush to seek quick guidance from worldly leaders, neglecting to test worldly leaders' insights against Kingdom values. They apply worldly solutions to spiritual problems. In contrast to Paul's encouragement to imitate leaders as they imitate Christ (see 1 Corinthians 11:1), they imitate leaders *instead of* Christ, and they propagate folly instead of wisdom.

Now, we must admit that there are things to gain from wisdom based on experience. But we must always filter these insights, conclusions, or principles through a Kingdom perspective. If one's leadership thinking aligns with the Scriptures (Kingdom thinking and values), then we accept it. But if it is contrary to God's truth as revealed to us in His Word, then we must reject it. Wise Kingdom leaders accept the Bible, God's inspired Word to us, as our final authority and our primary leadership textbook.

The law of the harvest applies to all: You will reap what you sow. We cannot lead in the way of the world and then expect a lasting spiritual harvest. We cannot expect God's blessing on the leadership of one who fails to solicit the otherworldly wisdom of God. As Paul wrote, "Do not be deceived: God is not mocked, for whatever one sows, that will he also reap" (Galatians 6:7).

WHAT IS GODLY WISDOM?

Godly wisdom is applying knowledge and understanding to life situations by considering what is pleasing to God. Our goals are measured against the ultimate goal: a life that ends with Jesus telling us "Well done, good and faithful servant."

We never "arrive" when it comes to wisdom. We can always grow in wisdom, for we encounter it in God Himself, who is infinite, and therefore the wisdom He offers us is inexhaustible.

Kingdom wisdom doesn't just happen; it must be pursued. We can ask God for it (see James 1:5) and He will give it to us because He has promised to do so. Therefore, even young people with limited personal experience can be considered wise if God has given them wisdom from above. This is what happened with Solomon. He acknowledged that he was young and inexperienced (1 Kings 3:7) yet boldly asked God for "an understanding mind to govern [God's] people" so he could "discern between good and evil" (1 Kings 3:9).

We can and should, regardless of our age and experience, learn godly wisdom from others. Wise spiritual mentors are invaluable to our development. They help us continue growing throughout our lives. As we age, our mentoring needs change, moving from a whole-life perspective to a more focused, targeted mentoring later in life. Asking others for help in your growth and development is wise. If you are beginning your spiritual journey, look for someone to disciple you, helping you to become a follower of Christ. If you are well established in your walk with Jesus, then look for someone who demonstrates spiritual wisdom in an area that you can learn from, someone who is strong and wise in a specific aspect of life that you feel you lack.

Every time I've asked a leader to mentor me in a specific area, they initially hesitate or refuse me outright. "I've never done that before," they say. "I'm not sure that's a strength of mine." "I'm not sure where to even begin." "I'm really busy." Don't be put off if you experience something similar. Simply suggest a regular time just to eat together (everyone must eat sometime). Buy the person's meal (you need to demonstrate that you are serious about this mentoring endeavor). All your mentor must do is come willing to answer questions; no preparation needed. Kingdom leaders have been preparing for this through their life and leadership. It's your responsibility to get from them what they already know.

When I meet with a mentor, I assume that it is my responsibility to glean from them the particular wisdom I need. I come with several prepared questions related to the subject that I need their help with. I take notes for further reflection later. I ask them to share with me any Bible passages that they think relate to this specific area, or what resources they recommend—books, articles, other people to talk with, and the like.

Spiritual, godly wisdom springs from the knowledge of God, His character, and His Word. This spiritual knowledge leads to spiritual understanding of how God works—the ways of God. And spiritual understanding translates into spiritual wisdom, the final application of our knowledge of God and His ways into our daily decisions. It is this spiritual wisdom that God gives to Kingdom leaders to help us accomplish His purposes in us and through our leadership. It arises from spending time with Jesus and His Word, being taught by His Spirit, and learning from others who have done the same.

The catalyst for turning spiritual knowledge and understanding into spiritual wisdom is the Holy Spirit Himself, who lives within those who know Christ. He guides us to truth, helps us discern root issues, provides creative solutions to problems, and seeks to glorify Christ in and through us. He will bring the help that Kingdom leaders need. In Luke 2:46-47, the Jewish religious leaders were amazed at Jesus' answers, given His age of twelve. It was no doubt a similar observation made about Peter and John when they were brought before the Jewish leaders, who "recognized that they had been with Jesus" (Acts 4:13).

Godly wisdom allows Kingdom leaders to accomplish God-given tasks in such a way that people thrive and God is glorified. They don't seek credit for any success because they acknowledge that success comes from Him. They thus share the spotlight with those who serve with them. Such leaders are attractive; people move toward them not because of their charisma but rather because they sense that God is with them. They willingly submit to that leader's influence.

THE PILLARS OF WISDOM

In Proverbs 9:1 we read, "Wisdom has built her house; she has hewn out its seven pillars" (NIV). What are the seven pillars found in the house of wisdom? We find them listed for us in the previous chapter in Proverbs 8:12-14 (NIV):

> I, wisdom, dwell together with prudence;
>> I possess knowledge and discretion.
> To fear the LORD is to hate evil;
>> I hate pride and arrogance,
>> evil behavior and perverse speech.
> Counsel and sound judgment are mine;
>> I have understanding and power.

Prudence, knowledge, discretion, counsel, sound judgment, understanding, and power: These are the pillars of wisdom. The first three are the close *companions* of godly wisdom; they are interlinked and are overlapping. The final four are the *competencies* that flow out of godly wisdom—manifestations of wisdom in the life of an individual.

Following these verses, we read, "By me kings reign and rulers make laws that are just; by me princes govern, and all nobles who rule on earth" (Proverbs 8:15-16, NIV). Here we see that wisdom is given to leaders for the outworking of their leadership responsibilities. Kingdom leaders must lead with godly wisdom for their leadership to be God-blessed and lasting.

The remainder of this book will explore these seven pillars (and includes a final chapter on godly wisdom in action). As you make your way through the book, be sure to test what you read against your experience and what God has revealed to you of His character and truth. The devotional reflection at the end of each chapter and the wisdom-development resources in the appendix will aid you in that process. You will grow in wisdom by pursuing it.

DEVOTIONAL REFLECTION

BIBLE REFLECTION

Read and reflect on the following passages about God's wisdom. Note any observations and practical applications that you can make in your own life and leadership.

- James 1:5

- Proverbs 8:10-15

- Matthew 7:24-27

PRAYER ITEMS

- Ask God to give you wisdom that comes from Him based on the promise of James 1:5.

- Are you intentionally developing yourself into a wise leader? Ask the Lord to show you how to be more intentional in pursuing godly wisdom.

PERSONAL APPLICATIONS

- Read and meditate on the book of Proverbs, especially chapters 1–9, asking God to show you specific applications of His wisdom to your daily life and leadership.

- Are you intentionally passing on to others the wisdom God has given you? Whom could you meet with in the next week to begin doing so?

Part One

THE COMPANIONS OF GODLY WISDOM

*I, wisdom, dwell together with **prudence**;*

*I possess **knowledge** and **discretion**.*

To fear the LORD is to hate evil;

I hate pride and arrogance,

evil behavior and perverse speech.

Counsel and sound judgment are mine;

I have understanding and power.

By me kings reign

and rulers make laws that are just;

by me princes govern,

and all nobles who rule on earth.

PROVERBS 8:12-16, NIV, EMPHASIS ADDED

WE BEGIN OUR STUDY by looking first at the three companions of wisdom: prudence, knowledge, and discretion. These three are said to "dwell together with" wisdom—that is, they are found near and accompany godly wisdom. They overlap and influence each other, helping to make a person wise as they go through life. A person with godly wisdom will often display these three in their relationships as they interact with others.

PRUDENCE

*I, wisdom, dwell together with **prudence**;*
I possess knowledge and discretion.
To fear the LORD is to hate evil;
I hate pride and arrogance,
evil behavior and perverse speech.
Counsel and sound judgment are mine;
I have understanding and power.

PROVERBS 8:12-14, NIV

Prudence is foresight and far-sightedness. It's the ability to make
immediate decisions on the basis of their longer-range effects.

JOHN ORTBERG

WE BEGIN OUR EXAMINATION of godly wisdom by looking at the first
of its three companions: prudence. Prudence is the avoidance of rash
behavior or speech, the good stewardship of available resources, and
the showing of tact in relationships. It is also the exercise of good
judgment, caution, or circumspection with danger or risk. Prudent
leaders foresee the consequences of today's decisions in the future,
both near and long-term.

Prudence is certainly needed if we are to lead with wisdom,
because prudence greatly influences decisions regarding people and

resources. It informs a leader's risk assessment as they seek to apply limited resources to seemingly unlimited opportunities. Prudence seeks to maximize every opportunity, leveraging resources toward opportunities with the greatest impact. Prudent leaders know that helping people contribute in their strengths and maintaining good, trusting relationships enable all to work together well.

In Proverbs 1:4, we read that Solomon's proverbs are "to give *prudence* to the *simple*." A person who is "simple" is "unsuspecting . . . naive, foolish, easily deceived, and led into evil."[1] Obviously, Kingdom leaders cannot be "simple" as they interact with the world and seek to accomplish their God-given mission. Threats abound, and history is littered with those who began well but failed to finish well. John Wesley's foundational verse—the covering for his great Methodist work in England[2]—is still true for today: We must develop prudence to become "wise as serpents and innocent as doves" (Matthew 10:16).

LEADERS WHO LACK PRUDENCE

People who lack prudence don't think very far ahead. Thus, they are often caught by surprise at their circumstances, and their life is mostly crisis management. They are frequently reactive rather than proactive in their decision-making.

These are the "simple" people Solomon refers to above. They seek short-term, simplistic answers to the complexities of life, ignoring the long-term consequences of decisions made today. They assume that the saying "Today's problems are yesterday's solutions"[3] is true for all. They fail to realize that some of today's problems could have been avoided by prudent action beforehand. They don't think systemically, failing to realize that a decision made in one area of life has impact and implications for the whole, both long- and short-term.

Those who lack God-given prudence may acknowledge that they can't be simple *and* be a leader. But instead of seeking prudence, they pursue *shrewdness*, relying on their own insight and judgment, believing that they know best.

A tension exists between godly prudence and human shrewdness. Human (worldly) shrewdness seeks to gain personal advantage and "win." Selfishness is at its root; it tends to be focused on short-term goals. Godly prudence wants to see God's Kingdom win and gain glory for Him. It wants to advance the gospel and His purposes, not our personal agenda. Such prudence tends to keep longer-term goals in view.

Life is fast-paced and only goes faster. Leaders lacking prudence can be so busy (or self-indulgent) that they fail to stop and reflect. Even when they are focused on their mission, they repeat mistakes because they fail to learn from others and their experiences. They always appear to be in a hurry. They assume a high-RPM lifestyle is normal and may find their significance in their busyness.

Leaders lacking prudence speak their opinions freely and publicly without realizing that their words will be remembered and quoted. They do a lot of talking and little listening or asking questions. Their leadership is modeled more by telling than by asking.

A lack of prudence in leadership can result in a failure to keep people informed about change. Such leaders are constantly putting out fires that could have been avoided with better, more forward-thinking communication. Sadly, a reactive, crisis-oriented leader may find a great deal of satisfaction in always addressing a major problem and seldom stop to ask if the problem could have been avoided had they been more prudent.

Leaders lacking prudence tend to see all opportunities as equally strategic in both potential and risk, and they may fail to discern the best opportunity for impact. Thus, they "scatter seed" broadly, blindly hoping that something will take root and bear fruit from their efforts. They tend to look down on slower-moving, more cautious decision-makers who investigate before acting. They associate decisiveness with fast decision-making, regardless of how much is at risk or what the potential outcomes—good and bad—may be. For these leaders, the important thing is action.

A lack of prudence leads people to assign work based on need, whether the work is a good fit or not. The task must get done, and because we are always in crisis, we must put our heads down and work harder. Team members are exhorted to "take one for the team" and "be good team players." But when mission continually trumps a person's best contribution, people feel like tools being used rather than valuable partners in accomplishing God's purposes.

Jesus Himself speaks these words in Revelation 2:1-5:

> To the angel of the church in Ephesus write: "The words of him who holds the seven stars in his right hand, who walks among the seven golden lampstands.
>
> "I know your works, your toil and your patient endurance, and how you cannot bear with those who are evil, but have tested those who call themselves apostles and are not, and found them to be false. I know you are enduring patiently and bearing up for my name's sake, and you have not grown weary. But I have this against you, that you have abandoned the love you had at first. Remember therefore from where you have fallen; repent, and do the works you did at first. If not, I will come to you and remove your lampstand from its place, unless you repent."

The church in Ephesus was busy doing the Lord's work; they were accomplishing their mission and persevering in their service. Yet, in their busyness of *serving* the King, they had forgotten to focus on their *relationship* with the King. The Great Commission had trumped the Great Commandment. Their lack of prudent forethought on the consequences of not abiding in the vine (see John 15) was beginning to have dire results. Any seeming fruitfulness would be short-lived, just as a branch not attached to a vine quickly shrivels and dies.

CHARACTERISTICS OF A PRUDENT LEADER

Prudent leaders have several characteristics that greatly influence their leadership. Martin Manser has identified six characteristics of prudence in the Scriptures.[4] Let's examine them.

Foresight and Caution

One characteristic of a prudent leader is their ability to assess risk well. All leadership involves some level of risk, because leaders are leading into an unknown future. They make decisions today that bear consequences in an unknown tomorrow. Nothing is 100 percent certain. We never have all the information that we want to make a "perfect decision" (as if that were possible).

We must discern when we have enough information to make a good, timely decision, given the circumstances. Rashness can lead one to assume that deciding now is better than waiting on more information. And we must agree that at times, especially in crisis moments, we must make decisions sooner rather than later. But don't confuse decisiveness with making fast decisions. Truly resolute leaders move forward only when they have the right amount of information to make the best decision. Once they have that information, they move forward, not delaying any further.

Ecclesiastes 9:4 reminds us that "a living dog is better than a dead lion." A prudent leader can assess when risk is too high and avoid the danger. Those who are not prudent move forward and suffer painful consequences. Proverbs 22:3 says, "The prudent sees danger and hides himself, but the simple go on and suffer for it."

When I was sent to Indonesia for my work with The Navigators, one of the big challenges was to learn the local language, a key to successful cross-cultural ministry. Progress toward fluency seemed glacial at times. In the slow slog of language school, we were often reminded: "Inch by inch, it's a cinch. Mile by mile, it's a trial." Rolling my Rs was particularly difficult. As I practiced my drills for the one-thousandth time, it was so tempting to think, *Oh well, that's good enough. I can get by without getting this down well. Why continue to work at this when there is so much to do right now?*

Perhaps you've heard some say that the number one cause for missionaries returning home is failing to get along well with other missionaries. Or maybe you have heard that the reason is sexual immorality or illness or cross-cultural stress. During our decade plus serving in Indonesia, I kept my own log on why missionaries returned home prematurely. From my observations, a foundational reason was failing to learn the language well. This manifested itself in many secondary issues in their lives and ministries that ultimately sent them home. But those who worked hard at language acquisition (not just those who were gifted in language learning) had a notable staying power. Thus, good language learning was a key leverage point for lasting cross-cultural impact, at least in our Indonesian context. With the help of prudence, I learned that the effort and patience of seeking language fluency would yield a much better outcome than any short-term convenience of not seeking to master the foreign language.

The impatience of youth often leads to short-term compromise, which has long-term consequences. The time I invested in learning the language paid off: My Indonesian friends experienced my effort as an honor, and they were more receptive to my influence on their lives.

Discernment

A second characteristic of prudence is discernment. Leaders are continually forced into situations where they must discern root issues and determine the best course of action in challenging and often ambiguous circumstances. The more responsibility a leader has, the more complex the issues one must address. Discernment is key to getting to root causes and addressing solutions that bring about lasting—rather than superficial, short-lived—change.

In leadership-team decisions where there are differing opinions, discernment is desperately needed to determine the best course of action. Personnel decisions especially demand discernment, as we seek to reconcile what is a best fit for the person with what is best for the work.

In Proverbs 14:15, we see a contrast between the simple and the prudent person: "The simple believes everything, but the prudent gives thought to his steps." The simple person "believes everything" and thus is easily deceived by appearances or the first report. The words of Solomon remind us, "The one who states his case first seems right, until the other comes and examines him" (Proverbs 18:17).

In contrast, the prudent leader "gives thought to his steps," reflecting and asking questions to gain a deeper understanding of the situation. Prudent leaders *act* rather than *react*. They take a deep breath, pause, and think before they act.

Many younger, less experienced leaders make decisions out of zeal rather than prudence. Waiting for more information or the right timing is confused with weakness. In fact, prudence is often derided as an excuse for timidity. Zealous people—especially young people—see action deferred as action denied. While zeal can be a very good thing, it can quickly degrade into rash behavior. As such, prudence is not only a wise approach to a problem but also a helpful check against rashness.

Someone has said, "There are good decisions and fast decisions, but there are no good, fast decisions." Like many modern proverbs, there are exceptions to the rule. But in general, fast decisions will be regretted over time. Have you noticed the sales tactic to encourage fast decisions?

"If you call in the next three minutes, you can get twice the amount . . ."

"Attention shoppers: In our jewelry department, for today only, we are offering you . . ."

"If you don't buy it now, I can't guarantee you that this car will still be here tomorrow."

"I have three others who are waiting to see this house today, so if you want it, you have first chance at it . . ."

Salespeople employ such tactics because they know that if we pause and let our emotions settle, we probably will not purchase the item. It takes self-control, courage, and faith to resist the impulse to act, trusting rather that if such action is appropriate, God will provide the opportunity again. And perhaps, when that opportunity reappears in God's perfect timing, we will end with better results.

Proverbs 19:2 reminds us, "Desire without knowledge is not good, and whoever makes haste with his feet misses his way." Some crises are of our own making, due to procrastinating or ignoring decisions until they become a crisis. But most decisions are not emergencies and can be thought through if we plan far enough ahead.

During our time serving in Indonesia, we saw many newly arrived missionaries make choices that did not reflect prudence. They were often independent, having little supervision on the field, and thus were left on their own when deciding about lifestyle, language-learning processes, how to relate to Indonesian nationals and the government, and so on. Their zeal for accomplishing God's mission would often override prudent long-term paths, and they would suffer for it. Many came and many went home after short stays due to poor choices and a lack of prudence in decision-making.

Knowledge

One of the privileges of leadership is access to information that is not available to everyone. How a leader uses this information can be wise or foolish. It's not so much that *knowledge* is a perk of leadership as it is that *a capacity for knowing* helps a leader carry out their responsibilities. For example, "advance knowledge"—early information about new initiatives, changes, or decisions that affect others— can be exciting and gratifying: Our egos love being the one with the inside scoop on what is about to happen. But advance access to information isn't knowledge; knowledge is the processing of information, which includes considering its potential impact and how to lead well based on that information.

Sometimes withholding information—not sharing it with others—is the most prudent course of action. To avoid needless panic or anxiety, to bypass fruitless second-guessing or outright mutiny, or to honor legal confidentiality agreements are just a few examples of when it might be best to keep your knowledge to yourself.

In most leadership situations, however, prudent leaders keep those they lead informed about what will happen rather than waiting for it to happen and then reacting. These leaders have also thought about possible scenarios and helped those they lead anticipate responses. For example, we see Jesus sending His disciples into the city to obtain a donkey for His entry into Jerusalem (Mark 11:1-6). He instructs them to anticipate questions about why they are taking a donkey that does not belong to them. They encountered this challenge as they untied the colt and accomplished the assignment because He had helped them prepare for what might happen.

Speech

A prudent leader knows when to speak and when to remain silent. Proverbs 12:23 says, "A prudent man conceals knowledge, but the heart of fools proclaims folly." Just because you have a thought does not mean that you have to share it.

Knowing when to speak is very important. In team decisions, it is often best to wait to share your thoughts, for a leader's speech can dampen further discussion. As a team leader, your opinion tends to carry more weight; thus others might hesitate to offer differing views. This is especially true of a younger, inexperienced team.

Proverbs 21:23 reminds us to guard our mouths: "Whoever keeps his mouth and his tongue keeps himself out of trouble." A prudent leader knows that due to their influence, their words will be remembered. They wisely choose to have few public opinions about a variety of topics. It is not that their opinions are bad, but a prudent leader wants to be remembered and quoted for strategic and mission-related discussions. Choose your public opinions carefully, especially if your leadership role is one of great influence.

For ten years, I traveled multiple times a year to various western European countries to raise up next-generation leaders for our work. Frequent contact and God's favor made this a fruitful experience. But I quickly noticed that my European friends loved to talk about politics, especially American politics. And they would talk about these things forever! Now they had access to an American insider who could help them make sense of the American political system. I needed to decide how much time we should spend on this important-but-not-strategic topic. Did I want to be known for my opinions about American politics or my passion for Jesus, the Bible, and Kingdom leadership? I chose to deflect questions to keep the focus on the reason I flew across the ocean!

A Disciplined Ego

Prudent leaders are lifelong learners. They know that God uses others, particularly mentors and supervisors, to help them become all that the Lord intends. Prudent leaders especially embrace correction and rebuke and grow from it. Rather than defend or explain, they listen carefully and accept what is true as the Lord gives them insight. Proverbs 15:5 says that "whoever heeds reproof is prudent."

We must be open and teachable to all, not just to some. Leaders can show a "selective teachability" in that they are willing to learn from some people, but not from others. Naaman was such an individual; he struggled with teachability (see 2 Kings 5). Naaman found it difficult to accept Elisha's counsel to wash himself in the Jordan River to be cured of his leprosy. But he wisely listened to the counsel of his servant and was healed. Perhaps his desperation to be healthy humbled him enough to listen to his servant, who simply repeated what Elisha had said in the first place.

Have you seen leaders take advice from more senior leaders but reject the same advice from their peers? We do want to consider the source of the advice. But it's not just the source—it's also the substance of the counsel. A spiritual leader can certainly misdirect us theologically or even morally. If we only consider the source and not the substance, we'll be inclined to defer to a leader's authority. Let's not dismiss counsel simply because it comes from a peer or accept advice because it comes from someone in a higher organizational position. Discernment is needed in both situations.

Management of Talents and Resources

Sometimes a leader's most prudent course of action still seems outlandish and risky. When Pharaoh had a series of dreams (Genesis 41), Joseph suggested building large granaries to store food during abundant times so there would be food during lean years. Pharaoh recognized the prudence of this suggestion, and Joseph was elevated to number two in the kingdom.

Now, to an outside observer, Joseph's suggestion of storing large amounts of grain during years of bounty may seem imprudent. What makes it prudent is that the coming years of famine were assured, because God had given Joseph the meaning of Pharaoh's dreams. God used Joseph to rescue the nation of Israel from starvation and preserve the lineage of the Messiah (Genesis 50:20). The man with the plan gets the job!

Jesus uses a similar scenario as a negative example: A farmer tears down his barns and builds bigger ones to store a bumper crop (Luke 12:16-21). What made Joseph prudent and the farmer foolish? We only know by revelation, but the application for a leader is to be prayerful and circumspect, and act on faith when faith is required.

Prudent leaders manage their resources well. Just about anyone can accomplish a mission given a large amount of resources compared to the size of the task. It is the prudent leader who can accomplish much with little. Prudent leaders recognize that they are stewards of God's precious resources, and as such, will have to account for how they managed His talents. They live and lead within their budgets, demonstrating prudent frugality and making the most out of little. Should they have an abundance, they continue to invest His resources wisely, looking to maximize return.

Whether they have limited or abundant resources, good stewards seek to apply these assets to the best opportunities and leverage them for maximum impact. Kingdom leaders are stewards of God's resources—which include God's people. The author of Hebrews, in fact, makes Christian leaders' responsibility to God the basis of their authority: "Obey your leaders and submit to them, for they are keeping watch over your souls, as those who will have to give an account"

(Hebrews 13:17). As leaders, this accountability to God should sober us and cause us to maximize our opportunities and invest in the potential of those whom we lead.

In Matthew 25, we read of a master who gathers his servants and entrusts them with differing amounts of starting capital. He instructs them to put his money to work while he is away. Note what the text says:

> He who had received the five talents went at once and traded
> with them, and he made five talents more. So also he who
> had the two talents made two talents more. But he who had
> received the one talent went and dug in the ground and hid
> his master's money.
>
> MATTHEW 25:16-18

After a period of time, the master returns, and the servants are called to give an account of their results. The first two servants report having added to the initial capital, and the master rewards the faithful servants for their good work. But the third servant rationalizes his inactivity because he was afraid of losing the initial capital. The master is very disappointed and chastises him for his disobedience. Although this third servant did not lose the starting asset, he failed to increase it.

Wise leaders want to grow the Lord's Kingdom, being prudent as to how and where to invest His capital (people, money, time, materials) for the greatest return. Kingdom leaders know they need prudence to lead wisely to accomplish His purposes. While some people hear the word *prudence* and think of caution and even timidity, prudent leaders can actually move boldly. Their prudence allows them to act with more confidence, because they've fully measured the risk, reward, and resources God has given them.

DEVOTIONAL REFLECTION

BIBLE REFLECTION

Read and reflect on the following passages regarding the wise use of prudence. Note particularly how prudence applies to life situations.

- Proverbs 12:23

- Proverbs 14:15

- Proverbs 22:3

PRAYER ITEMS

- Pray and reflect over your past two weeks of interactions with your coworkers. Are there any areas where you have not demonstrated prudence in your actions? What should you do about it?

- Ask God to search your heart for any instances where you have not been prudent with your words. What would He have you to do about it?

PERSONAL APPLICATIONS

- Are you managing your personal and missional finances prudently? Do you have a financial budget, and are you following it? Are you saving for the future? What should you do to be more prudent in managing your finances?

- Are you preparing yourself now for future leadership contributions? Are you maximizing your strengths? What can you begin doing today to develop yourself as a leader?

3

KNOWLEDGE

I, wisdom, dwell together with prudence;
*I possess **knowledge** and discretion.*
To fear the LORD is to hate evil;
I hate pride and arrogance,
evil behavior and perverse speech.
Counsel and sound judgment are mine;
I have understanding and power.

PROVERBS 8:12-14, NIV

THE WORLD OFFERS US an abundance of knowledge. We research it, codify it, put it into forms where it can be accessed and shared with others. For example: We know that water is made up of two elements, hydrogen and oxygen. A water molecule has two hydrogen atoms and one oxygen atom held together by atomic bonds (H_2O). With the combination of these three atoms, we have water. This basic knowledge will lead us to understand more about water as we gain more information and experience.

Knowledge is the accumulation of facts and information that you gather over time. It is the basic component from which understanding and wisdom are built. There is much knowledge in the world today, and with the advent of the Internet and smartphones, we have easy access to increasingly vast amounts of knowledge. According to one website, "269 billion emails [were] sent daily in 2017"! Every day, 4.3 billion Facebook messages are posted and four million hours of new YouTube content is uploaded![1] Today, our challenge is how to keep from being overwhelmed by the sheer amount of knowledge now available.

With this vast amount of knowledge comes an additional challenge: How do we sort truth from error? So much of what is posted as factual is simply opinion, or worse yet, made-up "facts." We must have a filter to help us sort fact from fiction, truth from error. We need to find our way through the maze of information overload.

Some information is morally neutral—it's not good or bad. It's just information, like the latest baseball scores, menu items at your favorite restaurant, or the colors in a rainbow. But some information has moral overtones and broad implications. For example, the divorce rate among married couples, pornography-addiction rates among Christian leaders, or demographic changes in culture all have significant societal implications. Kingdom leaders focus on information that furthers understanding, leading ultimately to applying wisdom in their life and leadership.

As we work through the data that assails us, we build from the mundane to the important—like sorting the spam out of our inbox. We then go to progressively more high-stakes aspects of knowledge: The inputs we seek out, the facts we're presented with by our direct reports, the crises that test our will and our aptitude—all need to be assessed against a biblical backdrop. The priority of Scripture is more pronounced when we've been a bit overwhelmed by the volume and scope (and gravity) of information we're required to process. This is where a growing, general familiarity with the Word of God so helps us.

Not all facts are equally useful. Certain information may not contradict the Scriptures, but it may not be helpful, either. Here focus and concentration serve us well. We can clutter our minds with a lot of useless information that creates a lack of clarity or even confusion. In contrast to this never-ending, unfiltered adding of more and more information, we can choose to focus on certain topics, building layer upon layer of depth. This concentration generates a multiplying effect as we take what we know and add to it again and again, going deeper each time we revisit the subject.

LEADERS WHO LACK KNOWLEDGE

Leaders who lack godly knowledge prioritize seeking data, gaining experience, or searching for precedent over pursuing God. They are often plateaued learners when it comes to spiritual matters. Little fresh thought arises from the Scriptures as they recycle old insights or others' ideas. They summarize someone else's predigested work with little indication that they apply it to their own life. They attempt to make up for their lack of depth in God's Word or their superficial relationship with Him through their zeal. These leaders are "all sizzle, no meat"—or, as they say in Texas, "all hat, no cattle!"

Having vast experience does not ensure great knowledge, understanding, and wisdom. It could simply mean the same experience has been repeated multiple times. For example: Knowing the value of leadership teams, a leader selects team members to help with the work. When the team fails to work well together, the leader is surprised. Rather than taking responsibility for the team's leadership and resolving to better match people to tasks in the future, the leader blames the team members. When the next team falls apart, too, the frustrated leader again blames the team. And so it goes, the leader never stopping to notice that he or she is the common denominator of the problem.

Leaders lacking knowledge often seek out others who agree with them. They take advice from those who will reinforce their presuppositions. Paul says that those who compare themselves with themselves are not wise (2 Corinthians 10:12). They lack discernment to see their circumstances or issues objectively. Contrarian voices are ignored (note how Israel rejected the voices of God's prophets) because they do not agree with the leader's assumptions. When such a leader is confronted on poor decisions or challenged in presuppositions, they might label those who speak up as "not a team player" and kick them out of a circle of trust.

Leaders who lack godly knowledge often do not demonstrate teachability born of humility. They are not lifelong learners in the truest sense. They may continue to grow, but only in a reinforcing loop of selective learning from those who are like themselves and agree with them. "I know what I know," they say. "Don't confuse me with facts." These leaders frequently display a critical spirit toward those who think differently. Their leadership involves a tone of criticism and creates an environment of critique, and opposing opinions are voiced in hushed conversations outside of their hearing. Instead of continuing to grow in knowledge, they become increasingly isolated from the truth.

Leaders who lack the knowledge of God, His ways, and His Word will come to their natural end. God will let them go, hoping they will turn back to Him. But the law of the harvest cannot be ignored. We will reap what we sow! Those who gain knowledge from the world rather than the Lord will "sow the wind" and "reap the whirlwind" (Hosea 8:7).

BUILDING DEPTH AND STRENGTH IN KNOWLEDGE

About a ninety-minute drive south of where we lived in West Java is a village of renowned knife and sword makers. One day, we visited the village for a family outing and watched in amazement as these skilled craftsmen worked the steel blades in white-hot forges. A few very experienced blade makers there specialized in creating Damascus blades, which are distinguished by their patterns of banding that look like the ripples of flowing water.[2] This pattern is created by folding the white-hot steel onto itself, pounding it together, cooling it, and then repeating the process over and over again. Well-made Damascus blades are prized for their beauty, strength, and ability to be honed to a razor's edge.[3]

Gathering knowledge little by little over time shapes and strengthens our thinking in much the same way a Damascus blade grows stronger each time the steel is folded upon itself. We build layer upon layer of knowledge and test what we know with real-life situations. We can grow strong in knowledge by supplementing our understanding of biblical truth with other sources (studying models both good and bad), and by testing our assumptions against new data we take in.

But becoming strong in knowledge is not enough. A good knife blade is both strong and sharp. So it is with knowledge. We must become strong in knowledge *and* sharp in its usage. By concentrating and focusing, narrowing the spectrum of our knowledge gathering, we can sharpen our thinking to a razor's edge. This will require discipline, as we must say no to some interesting resources to focus our learning in other areas.

This tension between breadth and depth must be wrestled with as we pursue knowledge. In my forties, I began focusing my learning on the subjects of leadership and developing leaders, areas related to my vocation and contribution. This meant that my Bible study, personal reading, Scripture memory, and personal mentoring became increasingly narrowed. My life became more and more like a Damascus blade of leadership as, little by little, knowledge about leadership was added layer by layer in my mind and heart.

I'm not suggesting that to become an effective Kingdom leader, you must focus on the same subjects I did. But you will want to begin concentrating your learning in areas of life and vocation that you live in regularly and that align with your God-given design. For me, it was leadership and developing leaders. For you, it will no doubt be different topics. Focusing on select areas builds depth and strength from which we can have a greater impact on others. Focus for impact!

THE BEGINNING OF KNOWLEDGE: FEAR OF THE LORD

Common proverbs are created to capture some of the worldly wisdom based on experiences gathered over time. For example, "Look before you leap," "A penny saved is a penny earned," or "The apple doesn't fall far from the tree" all catalog observed experiences. But they have no ability to determine right from wrong or good from bad; they simply operate on the assumption that *results are good*.

Information is a building block of the foundation of understanding and wisdom. Without knowledge (information), there is no understanding or wisdom. But knowledge alone will not help us lead a wise life that is pleasing to God. If we are not careful, much knowledge can lead to an elitist spirit, an "I'm better than you" attitude.

By contrast, Proverbs 1:7 states, "The fear of the LORD is the beginning of knowledge." This fear is not terror or something that drives us away from the Lord. Rather, it is respect—a healthy awe and recognition that God is our Creator, the one with no beginning and no end, Alpha and Omega, King of kings and Lord of lords. We are but dust whom He has breathed life into. Truth resides in Him and His Word, and therefore we focus our knowledge pursuit on knowing Him and His Word, with an eye toward applying it in God-pleasing ways.

Where is our ability to boast of our knowledge? Who created the human brain with its neural pathways and synapses that fire chemical connections, forming thoughts in our consciousness? Who enables us to store and recall memories? Who helps us sort out the myriad of details in our memories, arranging them into what we call *intelligence*? And who enables us to translate those thoughts into speech so that we can communicate them to others? It is God alone who gives us minds that can know. Nothing originates outside of Him. So where is the ground for our boasting?

Having knowledge helps us begin our journey to wisdom, but it is not the destination. Knowledge is desirable and good, but it is a contingent good—it is how we get to godly wisdom, the ultimate goal. When we covet knowledge for the sake of having it and consider the accumulation of knowledge the measure of our worth, we make it what it's not meant to be. We are idolizing knowledge for itself, which is in fact the opposite of godly wisdom—wisdom based in and begun from a fear of the Lord.

The knowledge that leads to godly wisdom is rooted in knowing God through His Word. It is knowing Him personally—intimately. It flows out of a growing, dynamic love relationship with Him over a lifetime. This knowledge results from pursuing God, loving Him with all your heart, soul, and mind (Matthew 22:37-38), and living a life pleasing to Him. It is the pursuit of God for the whole of life. In his prayer for the Colossian believers, Paul asked God that they "may be filled with the knowledge of his will in all spiritual wisdom and understanding, so as to walk in a manner worthy of the Lord, fully pleasing to him" (Colossians 1:9-10).

This God-based knowledge is

> to recognize him for what he is, the sovereign Lord who
> makes a demand on man's obedience and especially upon
> the obedience of his people Israel, with whom he has made a
> covenant. He is the God whose holiness and loving-kindness
> are "known" in the experience of nation and individual. The
> criterion of this knowledge is obedience, and its opposite is

not simply ignorance but rebellious, willful turning away
from God.[4]

Thus, knowing God means we gain perspective. We draw breath
and our heart continues to beat because He wills it. We worship
Him with "reverence and awe" (Hebrews 12:28-29) because He is
our Creator and Lord.

KNOWLEDGE AND OBEDIENCE

Just as knowledge and understanding are linked together, so, too, are
knowledge and discretion, and we see them frequently juxtaposed in
Scripture. Discretion is being sensitive in speech or behavior, avoiding
offense, and having tact. One cannot have discretion without first having knowledge (see Proverbs 1:4). Knowing God's Kingdom norms as
well as the cultural norms of our context allows us to influence others
wisely. Having a God-based knowledge allows us to differentiate right
from wrong, good from bad, eternal from temporal, and Kingdom-like
from worldly. We may not be able to totally avoid offense, but we can
relate to others knowingly rather than out of ignorance.

Gaining God-rooted knowledge requires that we are teachable
to God. He longs for us to listen carefully to Him and obey His
commands. He wants us to come through the trials of this life well,
bringing glory to Him as we do so. God instructs us, but we must
listen and apply what He teaches (Matthew 7:24-27). We listen with
our hearts and minds, attuning to His voice and separating it from
the cacophony of other voices in our world. We know His voice and
follow it (John 10:27-28).

This teachability to learn about God requires confidence in His
ability to speak from His Word. If the Bible is not the inspired,
authoritative Word of God, then I can pick and choose what to
believe and obey. Those parts that seem difficult to understand or

challenging to embrace, I simply ignore. For example, I like the parts about God's love and acceptance but find it difficult to accept God's justice and judgment.

If the Bible is the Word of God, then I must submit to its authority and teaching in all areas—those that I understand and like and those that I find difficult to logically embrace. This is not blind obedience but rather a true awareness of myself. I know that I don't know everything, and God knows a lot more than I do. I know that His ways are not my ways, nor are His thoughts mine (Isaiah 55:8-9). I know His character is unchanging and that whatever inconsistency or seeming injustice I perceive is due to my lack of complete knowledge and understanding of Him. I choose to continue pursuing Him through His Word and trust that as He reveals Himself to me, these areas of confusion and lack of understanding will disappear as I come to know Him better. In the meantime, I choose to fully trust and obey Him and His Word, to the best of my ability.

Three aspects of growing in godly knowledge are foundational for wisdom: knowledge of God Himself (His personality and character), knowledge of God's ways, and knowledge of God's Word. Let's look at these.

Knowledge of God

The knowledge that leads to discernment and ultimately to wisdom is based in knowing God's personality and character. The completeness of God is most clearly revealed in the personhood of Jesus Christ: "For in him the whole fullness of deity dwells bodily" (Colossians 2:9). He is "the image of the invisible God, the firstborn of all creation" (Colossians 1:15). Jesus Himself says, "I and the Father are one" (John 10:30). Jesus was God incarnate, taking the form of a man that He might ultimately identify and communicate with us. As we come to know Jesus, we grow in knowledge of God—His personality and Christlike character.

The felt need for many young, emerging leaders is for leadership-skill development. New responsibilities come with deadlines that must be met. Thus, we pursue competency development instead of character development because competencies are often linked to dates on a calendar. Tasks and responsibilities come with deadline demands, so our focus is on skill development to meet the deadline demands. There are no deadlines when it comes to character development. No one asks, "Have you reached some level of maturity in servanthood or humility?" Thus, character development is ignored or pushed aside to be addressed later. Addressing character growth never seems to be convenient or make it to the top of our to-do lists.

And when a leader successfully accomplishes a task, they are often rewarded with more responsibilities. A leader's reward is more leadership. These new responsibilities come with new tasks and new deadlines that demand new skills to be developed. And so it goes. With each new responsibility or task come new skills to be learned. A job well done is rewarded with new skills to be learned. We just never seem to find the time for character growth. Oh, we give lip service to its importance, but intentionally pursuing Christlike character growth never becomes a priority.

No one gives leaders a deadline for developing some aspect of their character. It is not in their job description or part of their annual review. The sad truth is that most leadership failure happens at the pinnacle of a leader's influence because of some character flaw, and almost never because of a lack of skills. This character flaw was there for some time, but it was overlooked or ignored in the hope that it would self-correct. As a leader grows in influence, the number of people affected by this weakness grows until finally, the leader has become the problem and must be removed.

Just getting older will not sufficiently help us grow in Christlike character. Growing in Christlike character must be pursued, and it must be intentional. The character of God is multifaceted. We cannot simply hope that we will grow in godly character from getting older and gaining life experience. Unfortunately, many older, experienced people are anything but Christlike!

Wise leaders gather skilled staff and team members around them to compensate for their lack of skill in an area. But character cannot be delegated! Leaders cannot staff a leadership team based on their own character deficiencies. Each team member should have the character qualities needed to support their leadership responsibilities. A wise leader, therefore, will intentionally develop godly character qualities, knowing that this will pay long-term benefits for them personally and for their leadership influence.[5]

As we come to know Christ, we come to know God Himself, His character and His ways. We discover who God is as He reveals Himself to us—the way, the truth, and the life (John 14:6). Because God is a God who works (John 5:17) and we are created in His image (Genesis 1:27), we, too, are to be a missional people who work to accomplish our God-given tasks. Our mission flows naturally out of our God-given design as we pursue Him with all our heart, soul, and mind.

Christ's followers are a people on a mission to disciple the nations (Matthew 28:18-20), empowered by Him who has all authority and who has promised to never leave or forsake us. God's missional people will develop life messages growing from their gifting and the God-given design that He intends to use for His purposes through them. These life messages will align with His purposes for us (Ephesians 2:10) that are our destiny as we live out His calling on our lives. As we grow to know Him, we discover our God-given purposes and align our lives accordingly.

Knowledge of God's Ways

A second aspect of godly knowledge that leads to godly wisdom emerges from knowing the ways of God. God's ways are found in looking at His patterns of dealing with mankind and are often summarized in Jesus' teaching—especially in the parables.

Some years ago, while studying the life and leadership of Moses, I came across several passages regarding Moses' requests of God (see Exodus 4:1-17; 33:7-22). He asked for help in speaking and God gave him Aaron. He asked to see God's face and the Lord graciously gave Him a look at His back side. Moses also asked God to "show me now your ways, that I may know you" (Exodus 33:13). Note that Moses' request to know God's ways was couched in the context of his leadership: "You have been telling me, 'Lead these people'" (Exodus 33:12, NIV). Moses saw that knowing God's ways was essential to success in leading God's people, so he asked God to teach him His ways. Moses realized that his leadership would overflow from his growing intimacy with God.

After completing that study, my personal application was like that of Moses. I also began to ask God to teach me His ways (if Moses thought it important, then perhaps I should too). I began to keep a special journal where I would record any of the "ways of God" as I discovered them over time. In keeping the journal, I intended to demonstrate to the Lord that I was paying attention to His teaching as He revealed Himself more clearly to me. As I discovered the ways of God, I also sought to apply them to my life and leadership.

Here are some examples of the "ways of God" that I have recorded, along with some of my personal applications.

- Kingdom growth begins small and over time becomes large (parable of the mustard seed—Matthew 13:31-32); therefore, do not despise small beginnings.

- God uses what the world does not value so that mankind cannot take credit for the results (1 Corinthians 1:26-31); therefore, do not be discouraged by an apparent lack of gifting or resources to accomplish His tasks, for it is in such circumstances that the power of God is manifested.

- God's timing is perfect from His eternal perspective, but from man's perspective, His actions often appear to be late (e.g., God waited until Abraham and Sarah's bodies were "as good as dead" before giving them a son—Hebrews 11:11-12); therefore, do not give God a deadline for when He must act or be anxious when His answers to prayer seem long in coming. Rick Warren reminds us, "God is never in a hurry, but he is always on time."[6]

God was faithful to answer Moses' request and did teach Moses His ways. We see David's testimony about this in Psalm 103:7: "He made known his ways to Moses, his acts to the people of Israel." Moses came to know the ways of God, but the children of Israel knew His acts. Anyone in Israel could also have known God's ways had they asked Him. Moses' intimate relationship with God led him to ask to know God more deeply. The tragedy of Israel was mishandling the knowledge they had been given, for what they knew of God was not born of the fear of God or of a growing intimacy with Him. It led them to grumble in the desert and to demand more from God than He was giving.

Knowing the ways of God means knowing the *why* behind God's actions. We know His motives and the values that drive God's behavior. Israel only knew the actions of God, but Moses knew God's purposes and His motives. By knowing the ways of God, leaders can align their leadership with His ways and further God's ultimate purposes.

Learning God's ways is gained through spending time alone with Him. Moses spent countless hours and days alone with God, speaking with Him as one friend speaks to another. Through this extended time together, Moses began to understand the purposes and motives of God's actions in dealing with His chosen people. As he grew in his relationship with his heavenly Father, Moses could better lead God's people in following the plans God had for them. We, too, can grow in our relationship with Him and learn the ways of God by spending time with Him in prayer and in His Word. This will not be a short-term project, but just as Moses spent forty years in the desert with God, we can spend a lifetime getting to know Him and His ways. God promises us that "You will seek me and find me, when you seek me with all your heart" (Jeremiah 29:13).

Knowledge of God's Word

Today we have the Bible as a primary means of hearing God speak to us. Just as Moses had the incredible privilege of spending time "face to face" with the living God (Exodus 33:11), we have access to His presence as we meet Him in prayer and spend time in His written Word. It is important that we view the Bible as a means to an end and not the end in itself. We spend time in the Bible to get to know the author of the book, not just to know the book itself. The Bible is a tool to help us know God personally, to know His ways and how He interacts with His people.

The Bible promises much to those who meditate on the Word of God. One of the greatest benefits promised to those who do so is gaining godly wisdom. God promised the following to Joshua: "This Book of the Law shall not depart from your mouth, but you shall meditate on it day and night, so that you may be careful to do according to all that is written in it. For then you will make your way prosperous, and then you will have good success" (Joshua 1:8). But success in the eyes of the world is different from success in the eyes of God. Living a successful life means living a life that is pleasing to God. Those who do so wisely choose to please God rather than the world. God's leader, Joshua, was promised success in whatever he undertook if he would but meditate on God's Word.

The psalmist promises,

Blessed is the man
    who walks not in the counsel of the wicked,
nor stands in the way of sinners,
    nor sits in the seat of scoffers;
but his delight is in the law of the LORD,
    and on his law he meditates day and night.
He is like a tree
    planted by streams of water,
that yields its fruit in its season,
    and its leaf does not wither.
In all that he does, he prospers.

PSALM 1:1-3

The promise still stands today for God's leaders who meditate on God's Word. Much of my prayer time is spent meditating and praying over Scripture passages. Some verses relate to various character qualities of God. Other passages are personal promises pertinent to my life, family, and ministry. I come to know Him more intimately through reviewing these promises in my mind and heart as I pray. By prayerfully reflecting on His Word, we can learn to hear His voice speaking to us as He reveals Himself in new and deeper ways. We will also find many applications to our life and leadership as we do so. Relationship is built on the foundation of spending time together—communicating with each other. And so it is as we pray and meditate on God's Word.

The Word of God is itself knowledge—a source of information alongside countless other artifacts available to us at any given moment. But the Bible offers facts about God, who is transcendent and without error. Through the voice of God, the Bible offers information about the world God created, including each of us. It is reliable, trustworthy, and infallible because it is God's very Word to us. What is our attitude toward God's Word? Do we approach it more as an academic text or as a life manual? Are our devotions a means for life-giving abiding in Christ, building deeper intimacy with Him? Is Scripture memory a means toward meditating on God Himself, seeking to think His thoughts and apply them to our life?

Some years ago, I was interacting with Dr. J. Robert Clinton about a personal goal to increasingly deepen my knowledge of the English Bible during my lifetime. After listening patiently and asking some questions, he offered, "Tom, I think you have an impossible goal."

"Why would you say that?" I asked.

"Because," he replied, "the Bible is not really one book; it is a library of sixty-six books. It's too much to try to master in one lifetime."

He could see my disappointment, and he quickly added, "But there is a better way to develop the depth you desire. Instead of trying to become proficient in the entire Bible, focus your effort around a Core Set of Bible books. Begin with four books: one of the Gospels, Romans, Ephesians, and another book of your choosing—one that you spend a lot of time in, one that you've marked a lot in your personal Bible, or the book where you have to tape the pages back together due to wear."

"Why Romans and Ephesians?" I asked.

"Because they explain Paul's two revelations from God—the gospel and the body of Christ," he said.

A Core Set, according to Dr. Clinton, is where we focus to build depth in our Bible knowledge. We have daily devotions in these books, we memorize verses from them, we read them repeatedly, we do personal study in them, and so on. The more influence and responsibility we have, the broader our influence, and therefore, the more books of the Bible we need in our Core Set.

Besides full Bible books, our Core Set may include select passages (e.g., Matthew 5–7, Romans 6–8, or 1 Corinthians 13), Bible characters (David, Esther, Mary, or Paul), or themes (leadership, leader development, disciple making, or holiness). Focusing in these ways will allow us to serve others from an overflow, an increasing depth of knowledge of God and the Bible.

Of course, while focusing on a smaller portion of the Bible, we need to stay familiar with the entire Scriptures. There is much profit in reading from the whole Bible (2 Timothy 3:16-17). Don't become so myopic that you miss great blessing. You wouldn't want to get to heaven and not have an answer if Nahum asks you, "So, how did you like my book?" You'd want a working familiarity with it so that you're not embarrassed to admit that you never found the time to read or study it.

Your Core Set will be a dynamic list. As God gives you more influence and responsibility, you'll want to add to it, and as you move through different seasons of life, your books and selected passages, characters, or themes may change accordingly. We can delete from our Core Set as well as add. We want to live and lead from an overflow of our walk with God. Concentrating in a Core Set has proved incredibly helpful for me and enabled me to deeply influence others as I serve others out of my focused study of Scripture.

Wise leaders fear God and pursue a growing intimacy with God through His Word. They lead from their growing knowledge of God, His character and ways, and the truth they discover in His Word.

DEVOTIONAL REFLECTION

BIBLE REFLECTION

Read and reflect on the following passages regarding godly knowledge. Note particularly how knowledge applies to life situations.

· Proverbs 10:14

· 1 Corinthians 12:4-11

· 1 Timothy 6:20-21

PRAYER ITEMS

· Pray over some of the Psalms or your favorite Bible passages related to God's character, asking God to help you know Him and His ways.

· Ask for God's guidance in applying His ways to your life and leadership.

PERSONAL APPLICATIONS

· God reminds us to "prepare [our] minds for action" (1 Peter 1:13, NASB). Are you facing a decision that you need to gather more data about before acting? If so, take whatever steps are necessary to get this additional information.

· Read and meditate on the book of 1 John. Note how the word *know* is used and what God would have us know about Him and about ourselves.

4

DISCRETION

I, wisdom, dwell together with prudence;
*I possess knowledge and **discretion**.*
To fear the LORD is to hate evil;
I hate pride and arrogance,
evil behavior and perverse speech.
Counsel and sound judgment are mine;
I have understanding and power.
PROVERBS 8:12-14, NIV

The better part of valour is discretion.
WILLIAM SHAKESPEARE

WE WILL NOW EXAMINE the third of the three companions of godly wisdom, that is, prudence, knowledge, and *discretion*. Discretion describes perceptiveness and cautiousness in speech and action— careful consideration of the circumstances and possible consequences of one's actions and influence.

Discretion includes the ability to anticipate a response during an interaction and choosing words carefully as a result. It does not mean that we avoid conflict, but rather that we are aware of possible responses to our words and deeds and are seeking to help, not to harm. Discretion involves *emotional intelligence*—the ability to monitor how our interaction is impacting all involved on an emotional level.

Jesus reminds us, "Do not give dogs what is sacred; do not throw your pearls to pigs. If you do, they may trample them under their feet, and then turn and tear you to pieces" (Matthew 7:6, NIV). Not everyone will be receptive to Kingdom truth. We must discern a person's level of receptivity and share accordingly. We must also ensure that they are wrestling with God's truth and not stumbling over our method of delivering this truth.

Paul demonstrated discretion when he told a Roman centurion that he was a Roman citizen and therefore could not be flogged without prior proof of guilt (Acts 22:22-29). When he was questioned about his ministry by the Sanhedrin, Paul also showed discretion. He realized that two groups with differing beliefs about resurrection stood before him, and said: "'Brothers, I am a Pharisee, a son of Pharisees. It is with respect to the hope and the resurrection of the dead that I am on trial.' And when he had said this, a dissention arose between the Pharisees and the Sadducees, and the assembly was divided" (Acts 23:6-7). Note Paul's ability to read his audience and shape the conversation with his response.

Discretion can be demonstrated by speaking, but it can also be demonstrated by remaining silent. When we do speak, we use discernment, carefully pursuing our desired impact on those around us by our choice of words.

Leaders are often asked for advice and counsel (we'll address wise counsel in the next chapter). When giving advice, it can be so tempting to tell all we know and have experienced over our entire journey with the Lord. And we can feel so compelled to tell everything now rather than let the process of growth and maturity run its course over time. A wise and discreet person will first ask themselves: *What does this person need to hear now?* What you don't say can have more impact than what you do share!

Discretion is foundational to leading with wisdom. It focuses awareness both internally and externally, keeping us conscious of our influence on those around us. Let's examine how wise leaders use discretion in their words and behavior.

LEADERS WHO LACK DISCRETION

Why would someone who normally uses discretion wisely occasionally not do so? The answer is that they lose control of their emotions. Perhaps from anger or in response to a perceived threat, they let their emotions lead them to very indiscreet behavior, and they say or do things that they later regret. Personal insecurity can lead to a fight-or-flight response to a perceived threat. If we choose the fight response, we will defend ourselves, often as we indiscreetly wound others with our words or actions. If we choose the flight response, we will either withdraw or hide our emotions, creating a duplicity between our outward actions and our inner feelings (our outward actions are those of a decisive, confident leader while our inner feelings reflect turbulence within). This duplicity, born of fear, can be deceptive and confusing for those we engage with.

Leaders who lack discretion can offend or upset those around them, often without even realizing it. They may use inappropriate terminology, tell offensive stories, or display mannerisms that turn off their audience rather than draw them in. For example, American culture is accustomed to casual clothing, even in professional settings. In Indonesia, one shows respect to others by the way one dresses when meeting them. In that context, casual dress can appear sloppy and conveys disrespect for those we meet. Discretion means adjusting your attire to avoid causing offense or distracting from the message you hope to communicate.

In America, we use formal titles like "Mr." or "Dr." when initially meeting someone, but as a relationship grows over time, we simply address people by their first name. In Indonesia, dropping a title is a sign of disrespect, regardless of how long the friendship has been established. Discretion means continuing to use these titles when referring to someone or addressing them directly.

Discretion acknowledges the potency of our words. Verbal processors lacking discretion can leave an audience with the impression that a *discussion* was a *decision*, when in fact, the conversation is (or should be) ongoing. Thus, verbal processors can give offense and even be accused of duplicity or outright deception because they said one thing to one conversation partner and something else to another. Verbal processors can avoid this confusion by leading with disclaimers like "I'm still in the process of thinking this through, but as of now, here's what I think . . ."

Leaders who lack discretion are more focused on themselves than on those around them. They are more concerned about being heard than about hearing from others. They want to talk rather than listen. They often tell instead of ask. I remember meeting with a leader who, when I sat down, asked me, "How are you, Tom?" Before I could begin to answer, he went on to explain how he was doing and what was happening in his world. The sixty-minute meeting ended with me never sharing anything, just listening to him ask and answer his own questions, completely unaware that I had mentally checked out about ten minutes into the "conversation."

When confronted with their offense, those who lack discretion will often adopt a defensive posture, explaining that it was not their intention to offend. Or they will transfer the blame to the offended, saying that they need to "get a thicker skin" or simply "grow up." Leaders who lack discretion rarely take ownership of their behavior and thus continue to create difficulties for those who interact with them.

REMAINING SILENT BECAUSE OF DISCRETION

Solomon reminds us: "Even a fool, when he keeps silent, is considered wise" (Proverbs 17:28, NASB). And Abraham Lincoln said,

"Better to remain silent and be thought a fool than to speak out and remove all doubt." Being discreet means knowing when to speak and when to remain silent.

Jesus demonstrated discretion and self-control when revealing Kingdom truth to His disciples. At the end of His public ministry, He reminded them, "I still have many things to say to you, but you cannot bear them now. When the Spirit of truth comes, he will guide you into all the truth" (John 16:12-13). Although there was so much more He could have shared with His disciples, it was not the right time. Jesus chose not to share with them but promised that at the proper time, the Holy Spirit would teach them the things that He longed for them to know.

When we went to Indonesia on behalf of The Navigators, we were allowed into the country on a student visa, and I was frequently asked why we moved our family halfway around the world to study the Indonesian language. What did we hope to do after finishing our formal language learning? Now, I could have said, "We hope to work as missionaries and share the gospel, with the intention of seeing Indonesian people come to faith in Christ." And that was indeed our hope—that the fruit of our efforts would be people coming to Christ. But especially given that Indonesia is the largest Muslim country in the world, mentioning that goal would have been less than discreet or prudent. Sharing the gospel is restricted in many countries like Indonesia, where Christianity is a minority religion, and certainly being indiscreet in our gospel mission would provoke the government, who, of course, would be our host in the country.

The answer I gave instead—"I'm not sure what we will do after language learning, as it will depend on the type of long-term visa that we're able to obtain"—was truthful, but discreet: I did not volunteer any unnecessary information that possibly could have created more difficulties. In this case, what I did not share was very important.

Discretion sometimes means that we don't share all things with all people.

There is a clear distinction between discretion and duplicity. *Duplicity* is speaking falsehoods—lying. It is saying one thing and then doing another. *Discretion* is always speaking the truth but knowing how much to share according to the context. Discretion thinks before sharing, anticipating possible consequences and then determining what to share or not share at the time.

Kingdom people are lovers of truth. Integrity is Christlike. Jesus was known as such a truth teller that His enemies tried to use it against Him in a hypothetical question related to paying taxes. They prefaced their question with this: "Teacher, we know that you are true and do not care about anyone's opinion. For you are not swayed by appearances, but truly teach the way of God" (Mark 12:14). Proverbs 11:3 reminds us, "The integrity of the upright guides them, but the crookedness of the treacherous destroys them."

SPEAKING UP WITH DISCRETION

Another feature of discretion is knowing how to share your thoughts in such a way as to be listened to and taken seriously. Younger, less experienced team members will often defer to the leader. This can be especially true in a culture that honors age and position. When discussing various facets of a decision with a team in this context, wait for team members to share their thoughts before weighing in with your own. When you do share your thoughts or opinions, invite others to disagree with you or share contrasting ideas. You can open with something like "I may not fully understand this, but from my viewpoint . . ." or "Based on what I see right now, I think . . . . I'm open to more of your thoughts on this matter."

Some of us may have a commanding presence, and our voice may carry a tone of self-assurance that almost dares others to disagree with us. It's not that we have an arrogant spirit; it's just the way our personality tends to come across. Being discreet means that we are aware of this possible "shutdown" impact on those around us when we speak. When we share our ideas, we do so with an intentionally softer tone of voice, adopting a less face-to-face, confronting posture but rather standing more at an angle to the person.

Discretion in speaking means that we consider the audience and how they will understand what we say. At times, Jesus was bold in confronting the Jewish leaders and their traditions, calling them "hypocrites" and "whitewashed tombs" (Matthew 23:27-28). At other times, He chose to patiently instruct them, as when Nicodemus questioned His identity (John 3:1-21).

Jesus was always aware of how His words affected those around Him. Note what He says at the raising of Lazarus:

> "Did I not tell you that if you believed you would see the glory of God?" So they took away the stone. And Jesus lifted up his eyes and said, "Father, I thank you that you have heard me. I knew that you always hear me, but *I said this on account of the people standing around*, that they may believe that you sent me."
> JOHN 11:40-42, EMPHASIS ADDED

Jesus was aware of the impact of His example and His words on those who accompanied Him.

When Paul spoke to the leaders of Athens on Mars Hill, he quoted a Greek poet to link their understanding of the "unknown god" to His message about Christ and the gospel.

> Paul, standing in the midst of the Areopagus, said: "Men of Athens, I perceive that in every way you are very religious. For as I passed along and observed the objects of your

worship, I found also an altar with this inscription: 'To the
unknown god.' What therefore you worship as unknown,
this I proclaim to you."

ACTS 17:22-23

Note Paul's awareness of the Athenian context as he tried to bridge
their acknowledgment of a god to Christ. Having observed their
numerous idols, he found the all-encompassing one to "the unknown
god," included in case they ignorantly overlooked some god. Paul
took this leaping-off point to introduce them to the Messiah. What
a wise person he was.

DISCRETION WHEN EXPLAINING OUR MOTIVES

Many times, leaders make choices or decisions that seem illogical to
others. We can then be confronted with questions as to our reasoning. At times, these decisions are based on more information than
what is available to others; thus, from our more complete picture, the
decision is logical. It gets more challenging when the information we
have is sensitive and not to be shared. Desiring to explain ourselves
or even defend our decisions can lead us to share more than we
should. We must exercise discretion in withholding some information, especially if it was given in confidence or would be damaging
if shared broadly.

Many personnel decisions may seem confusing at best to those
without access to relevant information. I remember having to fire an
employee for misusing authority. Due to the sensitive nature of the
issue and its impact on the staff person and those affected by their
behavior, we could not share details publicly. When this staff person's
dismissal became known, I was bombarded with numerous questions
of unfairness. It was so tempting to defend myself—I wasn't wrong-
headed, I was being a good shepherd leader. I was protecting the flock

and the overall work. But I could not share this sensitive information. I had to remain silent. What I did share was, "There is more to this decision than I am at liberty to share with you. Thanks for your understanding on this sensitive issue." Ah, the challenges of leadership!

DISCRETION IN BEHAVIOR

Discretion is also demonstrated by our actions. Like discretion in words, discretion in behavior means knowing when to act and when to wait. It also means that we are aware of the implications of our actions on those around us.

Jesus demonstrated discretion in His behavior while paying the temple tax.

> [Jesus said,] "What do you think, Simon? From whom do kings of the earth take toll or tax? From their sons or from others?" And when he said, "From others," Jesus said to him, "Then the sons are free. However, *not to give offense to them,* go to the sea and cast a hook and take the first fish that comes up, and when you open its mouth you will find a shekel. Take that and give it to them for me and for yourself."
>
> MATTHEW 17:25-27, EMPHASIS ADDED

Here, Jesus instructs Peter to pay the temple tax that He was rightfully exempt from. In this incident, Jesus did not want to offend those who were inquiring about it.[1]

Paul demonstrated discretion in speech and behavior when he realized that he would not get a fair trial before Festus and therefore appealed to Caesar, the highest authority in the Roman judicial system.

> Paul argued in his defense, "Neither against the law of the Jews, nor against the temple, nor against Caesar have I

committed any offense." But Festus, wishing to do the Jews
a favor, said to Paul, "Do you wish to go up to Jerusalem and
there be tried on these charges before me?" But Paul said,
"I am standing before Caesar's tribunal, where I ought to be
tried. To the Jews I have done no wrong, as you yourself know
very well. If then I am a wrongdoer and have committed
anything for which I deserve to die, I do not seek to escape
death. But if there is nothing to their charges against me, no
one can give me up to them. I appeal to Caesar."

ACTS 25:8-11

Paul's integrity is so strong that he willingly chances his life to
uphold his principles. He not only rejects Festus's offer to an unfair
trial but also does so discreetly. Such impressive restraint under pressure reveals that displaying discretion is not limited to speech; it
extends to actions, as well.

Another way to be discreet is through choosing attire that reflects
the wearer's modesty. Paul reminds Christian women that they should
exercise discretion in how they dress. "Likewise, I want women to
adorn themselves with proper clothing, modestly and discreetly, not
with braided hair and gold or pearls or costly garments, but rather
by means of good works, as is proper for women making a claim to
godliness" (1 Timothy 2:9-10, NASB). Here, the issue is being sensitive to those around you who are not as wealthy. Do not flaunt your
wealth or put your hope in it (1 Timothy 6:17-19). Rather, dress with
discretion, knowing that others are not as fortunate and your dressing
in a luxurious manner may lead to a focus on the wrong things in life.

Paul and Barnabas went to Jerusalem to convince the leaders of the
church that one did not have to follow the Jewish Old Testament law
to be a follower of Christ (Acts 15). Yet, when Paul recruited Timothy
to join him on his second missionary tour, he decided to have Timothy
circumcised. He did this because many knew that Timothy's father

was a Greek. Paul was not being duplicitous—rather, he was exercising great discretion, knowing that Timothy's heritage could become an issue for Jewish people as he accompanied Paul into Jewish places of worship. We know that very issue became the reason for Paul's arrest later, when he visited the Temple in Jerusalem.

> When the seven days were almost completed, the Jews from
> Asia, seeing him in the temple, stirred up the whole crowd
> and laid hands on him, crying out, "Men of Israel, help!
> This is the man who is teaching everyone everywhere against
> the people and the law and this place. Moreover, he even
> brought Greeks into the temple and has defiled this holy
> place." For they had previously seen Trophimus the Ephesian
> with him in the city, and they supposed that Paul had
> brought him into the temple.
>
> ACTS 21:27-29

Discretion is foundational for leading with wisdom. Being aware of our words and actions and how they influence those around us will help us avoid much misunderstanding and increase the impact of our leadership.

DEVOTIONAL REFLECTION

BIBLE REFLECTION

Read and reflect on the following passages regarding the wise use of discretion. Note particularly the applications to life situations.

- Proverbs 2:11

- Proverbs 11:22

- Matthew 7:6

PRAYER ITEMS

- Ask God to teach you discretion before you speak and to help you grow in awareness of how you affect those around you after you speak.

- Pray over the next two weeks of your schedule. Ask the Lord to show you where you can proactively prepare for and demonstrate discretion in these coming events.

PERSONAL APPLICATIONS

- Begin leading with verbal disclaimers as you share your opinions with others. Do this especially when sharing with team members and those closest to you.

- Give someone permission to tell you when they perceive a lack of discretion on your part. Enlist their help as you grow in self-awareness of this important quality.

Part Two

THE COMPETENCIES OF GODLY WISDOM

I, wisdom, dwell together with prudence;

I possess knowledge and discretion.

To fear the L{ORD} is to hate evil;

I hate pride and arrogance,

evil behavior and perverse speech.

Counsel *and* ***sound judgment*** *are mine;*

I have ***understanding*** *and* ***power***.

By me kings reign

and rulers make laws that are just;

by me princes govern,

and all nobles who rule on earth.

PROVERBS 8:12-16, NIV, EMPHASIS ADDED

In Proverbs 8:13, the flow of thought regarding the seven components of wisdom appears to be interrupted by an interlude. But it serves to divide the components of wisdom into two groups. The first three components are wisdom's *companions*; they develop along with wisdom in an individual's life. The four components after verse 13 are *actions*—products of wisdom in the life of a leader. In verse 13, the personification of wisdom reminds us that wisdom has a moral and a behavioral component.

We now continue studying the components of God's wisdom by looking at its four competencies: counsel, sound judgment, understanding, and power. These are often demonstrated in leadership contexts as we lead the mission, care for those we lead, and develop those people for greater contribution. A person with these competencies of godly wisdom will be skilled at leading in a way that pleases God.

5

COUNSEL

I, wisdom, dwell together with prudence;
I possess knowledge and discretion.
To fear the LORD *is to hate evil;*
I hate pride and arrogance,
evil behavior and perverse speech.
Counsel *and sound judgment are mine;*
I have understanding and power.

PROVERBS 8:12-14, NIV

To what greater inspiration and counsel can we turn than to the
imperishable truth to be found in this treasure house, the Bible?

QUEEN ELIZABETH II

WE TURN OUR attention to the four competencies of wisdom in the life of a leader: counsel, sound judgment, understanding, and power. The first of these is the ability to provide counsel.

By *counsel* we mean advice, human or divine. In the Scriptures, "although private individuals gave advice, professional advisors also existed. They included diviners like Balaam, courtiers (Joseph, Daniel), parents, and teachers. In wisdom literature, the word for 'counsel' became a technical term (Jer. 18:18; Prov. 8:14)."[1] Giving counsel to leaders was a respected function, and leaders sought wise counsel before making major decisions.

LEADERS WHO LACK WISE COUNSEL

Unwise leaders make decisions for others instead of letting them make decisions themselves. Many do so out of good motives, wanting to truly help others. A frequent outcome of this behavior, though, is that the counselors are blamed for the consequences when things don't go as hoped. Those giving the counsel then defend their actions or explain them away, saying they aren't responsible for others' actions. But if we are honest, we frequently *are* responsible because we greatly influenced others by our own example or counsel. We must own our influence as leaders—when things go well and especially when they don't!

Unwise leaders who lack godly counsel love to tell others what to do instead of letting them own their decisions. This satisfies their own need for feeling important, controlling others, or gratifying an overinflated ego. It's a power trip! But wisdom is "justified by [its] deeds" (Matthew 11:19), and the results of their lives and leadership decisions (including the decisions they make for others) will expose their folly.

Conversely, leaders who lack wisdom will fail to seek the counsel of others. They will take counsel from themselves only, perhaps not discerning that circumstances are different now than in previous situations they've experienced. When given sound counsel from others, they ignore it, trusting their own logic and understanding instead. They fail to consider that others may have more up-to-date data, greater insight, and Spirit-given discernment to help them make better decisions.

Consulting unwise sources for advice is another frequent mistake. Many sources have the outward form of wisdom but lack the source of true wisdom from the Lord. The advice many of these sources follow is contrary to the Word of God, and they experience the results of their lack of obedience. Such worldly wisdom may contain just a sprinkling of truth to make it seem plausible or right. But in the end, it does not lead to paths of righteousness or align with Kingdom purposes or values. Instead of following God's counsel, they do what is logical from the world's viewpoint.

Servant leadership is a trendy topic today. Certainly, Jesus had much to say about this very important topic (see Mark 10:42-45). And today in the marketplace, leaders are encouraged to model servant leadership. Many companies define servant leadership by what a leader does (e.g., parking far from the office's front door, turning the organizational chart upside down, doing menial tasks not usually associated with people of status). But the goal of business is to make a profit—to be successful—so if servant leadership doesn't contribute to that success or if it cuts into profits, it will be jettisoned and another theory tried.

For Kingdom leaders, being a servant is an identity, not an activity. Philippians 2:6-7 reminds us that "though he was in the form of God," Jesus "did not count equality with God a thing to be grasped, but emptied himself, by taking the form of a servant." Kingdom servant leaders sometimes express their servanthood by leading others. Other times, they express this identity by following another's leadership. The identity does not change; only the expression of service changes.

When we hear the phrase "Well, everyone else is doing it!" it should give us pause. There may be times when what is trendy can help us learn from another's experience. But we must be cautious, especially in moral issues. Those who follow the crowd in doing evil are unwise (Exodus 23:2). A type of pragmatic ethics can arise from relying on logic instead of God's absolute truth as found in the Scriptures to guide our moral decisions. It is not that the Lord wants to frustrate our lives by placing boundaries for our behavior. He came that we might experience the abundant life in its fullness (John 10:10). Boundaries are given for our protection and blessing, not as hindrances to joy and happiness. They serve as guardrails keeping us on the highway of God's righteousness, which leads to a fruitful life.

Many leaders fail to heed the warning signs of godly counsel and reap the harvest of their avoidance. They think that they are the exception, that they are special, and that the rules don't apply to them. Their short-term wins and apparent successes seem to justify their actions. But as long-term consequences begin to emerge, the folly of their choices and their detrimental impact on others makes it more apparent that they chose poorly.

LEADERSHIP AND WISE COUNSEL

Leaders are often looked to for advice. It is a wonderful privilege to truly help another by pointing them to the Lord and His Word as we give godly counsel. There is also a trap to avoid.

Our inflated egos often drive us to offer our own thoughts and commentary instead of His thoughts. Rather than referring others to God's Word for the best counsel, we share our own experiences and insights without referencing the Bible. Our experiences can be used to illustrate wisdom from His Word; in fact, this real-life application builds authenticity when counseling another. But it should never substitute for God's thoughts as recorded in Scripture.

More than once, I've been approached with this opening statement: "Tom, you seem so wise. Could you please give me your thoughts about . . . ?" Now, this request certainly appeals to my ego. *Why, how good of you to notice*, I think to myself. *You've come to the right source*, my pride echoes in my heart. And perhaps I have something to offer based on biblical insight or some pertinent previous experience. But if I'm not careful, my inclination is to share my insights and experiences and to draw attention to me.

All people like to be affirmed, and leaders are no exception. It's nice when someone acknowledges our strengths, hard work, and accomplishments. But we must remember how we got those strengths, who gives us the ability to work hard, and who creates opportunities to accomplish tasks and achieve our mission. We are reminded in 1 Corinthians 4:7, "For who makes you different from anyone else? What do you have that you did not receive? And if you did receive it, why do you boast as though you did not?" (NIV). This perspective allows us to accept recognition without inflating our ego.

A better approach would be to lead with something from the Bible, if appropriate. The Word of God is the good seed that brings forth growth. You will not always be available to help, so teaching and modeling that the Bible has a lot of relevance for their lives and leadership, that the Holy Spirit will help them find truth and application for their pressing issues, will serve them best long term. Having established a biblical context for the issue, you then can illustrate from your own thoughts or experiences how you addressed a similar situation. But don't let your ideas trump God's ideas by the emphasis with which you share.

Giving wise counsel is an art to develop. It involves listening well, asking questions for insight and discernment, trusting God for solutions to difficult problems, and walking by faith after reaching decisions. Those who mentor others must be excellent counselors—not in the clinical sense of counseling the hurting or broken but in the sense of guiding another person's growth and development. Those who possess wisdom are often (though not always) recognized by others and thus sought after for advice.

Leaders are frequently asked to solve problems that are too difficult for another person to solve. They are frequently asked for help because they have authority to make the exception or decide between two pathways of equal validity. Counsel that will truly resolve an issue or at least move forward toward its resolution must be rooted in wisdom from above.

Not every issue is necessarily a biblical one. For example, should we open a new ministry initiative in this city or that? What makes one a better, wiser choice than another? Our strategy would have a lot to say about which city we choose. The Bible helps inform and shape our strategy and the process by which we arrive at a strategic decision, not necessarily the decision itself. But when choosing members of a ministry-leadership team, we'd want to have some clear criteria, especially in moral behavior, because of the influence and tone they would set in the ministry. Here, the Bible clearly has a lot to say about qualifications for leadership.

COUNSEL IN DECISION-MAKING

Decision-making often falls within the purview of leaders. Good decisions are made when we seek and listen to counsel from other wise people. We are continually encouraged in the Word to seek counsel. No one person has the full perspective on a given situation. It is one thing to give counsel, but it is quite another to willingly receive it from others, especially if it runs counter to our ideas or conclusions. Wise leaders know how to both give and receive counsel.

Unless one leads by autocratic style, leadership decisions are made in the context of others—specifically, a leadership team. Let's suppose an issue is raised that requires a decision from the team. Background related to the issue is presented and possible outcomes are discussed. Depending on the complexity of the issue, various ideas are presented with supporting thoughts clarifying the best options for a path forward. Finally, a decision is made, with thought given to consequences and how this decision will be communicated and implemented.

As a team leader, one of the greatest challenges is knowing when to weigh in on the decision-making discussion with your own counsel—that is, your thoughts, opinions, and suggestions on the best way forward. Let's assume that your team members are aligning around a decision that you sense is unwise. How you speak into this situation, making sure that you address the issue and not the person, is key to keeping healthy team dynamics. Questions that you, the leader, raise can put people in defensive postures as they explain their reasoning. If they are somewhat insecure, being questioned by a leader on their position or ideas can either shut them down or cause them to over-react in personal defense. Even though you may simply seek clarity and better understanding, insecure team members may take your questions as a personal attack if they have difficulty in separating their ideas or opinions from their personhood. How you phrase the questions is important. It is not only *what you say* in your questions but *how you say it* that matters!

I remember leading a team discussion on an important personnel decision that we had to make. We didn't reach any kind of agreement on the issue after an hour of intense discussion. I listened to the discussion move back and forth around the table, watching veins stand out on team members' temples as their faces flushed with emotion. There seemed to be no end in sight.

My frustration was building as I thought about the many other agenda items of this multi-day meeting that needed just as much attention as this one. We had so much more to do. With one more comment, I'd finally reached my point of exasperation. "Enough already! We need to make a decision on this," I exclaimed. "After listening to all sides, here's what I believe we must do." My tone was anything but inviting for diverse opinions. No doubt my own veins were standing out and my face was crimson with emotion.

This team was a mix of young and old, experienced and novice. The young members shrank back into their seats, like turtles pulling their heads into their shells. And those who were older sat up straight and were ready to engage in a confrontation. It was a classic fight-or-flight response to a threat. And I was the threat! *This is not going to be pretty*, I thought.

My counsel was not well received. I had reacted instead of acted. While the move for closure may have been right, how I sought to move the team to that decision was wrong. Fortunately, a wiser team member quickly spoke up: "Why don't we just table this discussion for now? Let's pray about this overnight and come back to it tomorrow to see what the Lord has said to us about this issue." That was wise, godly counsel. We tabled the decision until the next day and, after taking a break, moved forward with other agenda items.

After letting that decision sit overnight, we came back to it the following day. Our emotions had settled by then, and clarity of thought quickly appeared. We shared new perspective we had gained from the Lord, and we were able to quickly reach a decision. Thank You, Jesus!

GIVING COUNSEL

Proverbs 18:13 reminds us, "If one gives an answer before he hears, it is his folly and shame." It is wise to make sure you understand the situation you are being asked to address before answering. After listening carefully, a good initial response is "So, what would you like from me in this situation? What are you expecting from our time together?" Some people may just want you to know of their situation and pray with them about it. Others may simply want you to listen and not do anything. They may be verbal processors who just need to talk it out with someone to help them clarify their own thinking about the issue. Ask questions for clarity and understanding, gathering context and history, and make sure you fully understand what you are being asked to give your counsel about.

One of my favorite questions is to ask is "What other counsel have you already received regarding this issue?" It could be that you are the tenth person that they have talked to and they hope to find someone who will agree with them instead of giving additional counsel that disagrees with their desires.

At times, someone may want you to decide for them. This frees them from responsibility or from owning the consequences of their decision. They can then come back later and say, "But you told me to . . ." Resist the temptation to decide for them. Don't let them manipulate you by saying something like "If you were me, what would you do?" Point them to pertinent principles in God's Word. Suggest possible solutions and potential consequences, if possible. Then let them wrestle with the decision themselves and bear the responsibility for its effects.

An exception to this rule is when the decision someone is facing is clearly a sin issue. In this circumstance, we do tell them what to do. Don't give in to temptation to sin! Resist the devil! Obey God! Warn them of possible consequences should they not obey. Don't leave them to figure things out on their own when the choice is between sin and righteousness.

We must be clear on differentiating between sin matters and differing personal convictions. For example, say someone asks your counsel on whether it is appropriate for Christ followers to serve in the armed forces. For many, this is not a sin issue, but for those with pacifist convictions, it is. Or should you serve alcohol at team-meeting meals? The Bible distinctly labels drunkenness as sin (for example, see Galatians 5:19-21). But what about drinking? One person's conviction is another's sin issue. In Romans 14, Paul addresses these disputable matters, drawing principles from the question of whether Christians could eat meat, especially meat used in pagan-worship services. When giving counsel on matters with divided opinions, we would be wise to apply the principles of this chapter.

GIVING COUNSEL IN MENTORING

When mentoring another, we frequently find ourselves enmeshed in their daily lives and challenges. It is so tempting to simply tell them what to do, especially if we have experience that relates to their context. We want them to avoid life's pain, and we hope to accelerate their growth to maturity by helping them avoid some of life's pitfalls. We sometimes forget that the process of growth is just as important as the outcome.

When giving counsel regarding life situations, it is important to ask yourself, "Is this an above-the-waterline issue or a below-the-waterline one?" Above-the-waterline issues are those that won't put the "ship" in jeopardy of sinking if things go poorly. Yes, there may be damage, but their individual life or leadership will not be irreparably harmed because of it.

Perhaps you've delegated a responsibility and the planned execution of it seems less than optimal based on your past experience. You could intervene and suggest a better way of doing it. But perhaps the best thing to do is let the person go forward with their plans and stay close enough to help if needed. And don't be surprised when their plans go better than you expected, as the Lord supports them and their efforts! The task or mission gets done, and the person learns much as you help them reflect on their experience and arrive at good conclusions.

By contrast, below-the-waterline issues are those that can sink a ship (person or mission) if things go poorly. These things can do great harm to the person or those they lead or cause the mission to fail. These issues need to be addressed carefully, warning those we coach of the seriousness of the issue and potential harmful consequences if the outcomes don't go as hoped. But even here, we must let those we mentor make their own decisions and live with the consequences. If you know that an action will greatly affect the greater mission, then you must insert yourself and stop the action for the greater good. A shepherd leader is responsible for both the individual sheep and the whole flock.

Sometimes we are not exactly neutral in the situations where we are asked to give our counsel. We can hope for a person to follow a certain path. When doing so, we must acknowledge to those we coach that we are not unbiased in our counsel and tell them that it may be hard for us to give totally objective advice. We can still give our counsel, helping them see advantages and disadvantages of the decision and perhaps anticipate some consequences. But again, we must let them decide for themselves. We must assure them that whatever they decide, whether it is what we hope for or not, our relationship will not be affected by this decision. Whatever way they choose, we are still for them and want to help further God's purposes in their life, as we are able.

I am often involved in recruiting people to consider whether God would have them pursue a career with The Navigators. Deciding one's vocation has huge consequences in the lives of those I counsel and recruit. As a Navigator leader myself, I can speak from my own experience about how I wrestled through that decision to leave my career in veterinary medicine to follow God's personal calling to work with people instead of horses. As I interact with new staff candidates, I must share that I am not totally objective in my counsel. I know the process that they are engaged in as they seek God's will in this very important decision. I'll show them how to discern God's calling in their life, but then I must leave the outcome between them and the Lord. Should they decide that He is leading them to The Navigators as their next step, I'll celebrate with them. But should He lead them to a different path, I will also celebrate that decision with them, knowing that His calling is unique for each of us. Serving as a vocational Christian worker is *not* best for everyone. It is only best for those whom He calls to it.

RECEIVING COUNSEL FROM OTHERS

It's one thing to give advice, but it is another thing to be able to receive it from others. Experienced, mature leaders sometimes adopt an attitude of "been there, done that," and this attitude hinders their ability or even their desire to seek and receive advice from others. As King Solomon wrote, "Better was a poor and wise youth than an old and foolish king who no longer knew how to take advice" (Ecclesiastes 4:13).

Wisdom, guidance, and success are found in having an abundance of counselors (Proverbs 11:14). Proverbs 15:22 says, "Plans fail for lack of counsel, but with many advisers they succeed" (NIV). Note that it does not say that these truths apply only to the young and inexperienced! All of us—regardless of age, maturity, or experience—still need the advice of others. We are reminded to seek counsel from several people, for some may give us bad counsel and others may not risk the relationship to tell us the truth. Through consulting several counselors, we will begin to see a way forward.

It can be especially difficult for husbands to receive advice from their wives. Our egos, bravado, and just plain stubbornness will not allow us to accept their wise advice. We ignore this counsel to our peril! Wives are a gift given to husbands as helper-completers in carrying out God-given tasks.

I was once with an older man driving through congested, crazy traffic in downtown Singapore. As a new, young missionary, I wanted to avoid the painful mistakes of my elders. So I asked this wise leader to share advice he wished he had been given when he was my age, something that would have served him well had he applied it in that season of his life. Without hesitation, he applied the brakes, and, with horns blaring and other drivers' voices raised, he pulled the car quickly to the curb. Turning off the engine, he put his finger in my face and exclaimed, "Tom, listen to your wife!"

It was some of the best (and certainly some of the most dramatic) advice I've ever been given.

The ability to give and receive wise counsel enables Kingdom leaders to further God's purposes in them and through them. Listen carefully to the Holy Spirit within you. He is the Counselor given to help you sort truth from error and know which way to go when you are confused. Jesus promised us: "I will ask the Father, and he will give you another Counselor to be with you forever. He is the Spirit of truth" (John 14:16-17, csb).

DEVOTIONAL REFLECTION

BIBLE REFLECTION

Read and reflect on the following passages regarding giving and receiving wise counsel. Note particularly the applications to life situations.

- Psalm 1:1-3

- Proverbs 12:15

- Proverbs 15:22

PRAYER ITEMS

- Ask God to counsel you from His Word as you seek to make any life decision. Ask for His guidance as you face decisions with multiple options.

- Ask God to teach you how to give wise counsel, especially how to give counsel from the Bible.

PERSONAL APPLICATIONS

- List some of the major questions or challenges that you are facing in this current season of life. Who can you ask for counsel related to these? (Hint: Consider someone at least ten years older who has successfully gone through this season.)

- Give someone permission to warn you when you seem unwilling to receive advice. Engage their help with growing in this important quality founded on humility and teachability.

6

SOUND JUDGMENT

I, wisdom, dwell together with prudence;
I possess knowledge and discretion.
To fear the LORD is to hate evil;
I hate pride and arrogance,
evil behavior and perverse speech.
*Counsel and **sound judgment** are mine;*
I have understanding and power.

PROVERBS 8:12-14, NIV

Good judgment comes from experience, and a lot
of that comes from bad judgment.

WILL ROGERS

SOLOMON WAS A YOUNG, inexperienced leader when he replaced his father, David, as king. He was aware of his need for wisdom to lead well and thus was inclined to ask God for help. Note his prayer for wisdom that would enable him to lead the people of Israel.

"Now, O LORD my God, you have made your servant king in place of David my father, although I am but a little child. I do not know how to go out or come in. And your servant is in the midst of your people whom you have chosen, a great people, too many to be numbered or counted for multitude. Give your servant therefore an understanding mind to govern your people, that I may discern between good and evil, for who is able to govern this your great people?"

It pleased the Lord that Solomon had asked this. And God said to him, "Because you have asked this, and have not asked for yourself long life or riches or the life of your enemies, but have asked for yourself understanding to discern what is right, behold, I now do according to your word. Behold, I give you a wise and discerning mind, so that none like you has been before you and none like you shall arise after you. I give you also what you have not asked, both riches and honor, so that no other king shall compare with you, all your days. And if you will walk in my ways, keeping my statutes and my commandments, as your father David walked, then I will lengthen your days."

1 KINGS 3:7-14

After Solomon decided who was the true mother of a disputed baby, we are told, "When all Israel heard the verdict the king had given, they held the king in awe, because they saw that he had wisdom from God to administer justice" (1 Kings 3:28, NIV).

By *sound judgment* we mean "efficient wisdom,"[1] wisdom that leads to practical application and success in problem-solving. "Sound judgment is based on the righteous character of God's rule. The upright have sound wisdom hidden in them (Prov 2:7)."[2] Sound judgment is closely linked to discernment—the ability to see strategically, discover root issues, and determine cause-and-effect relationships. Note that Solomon prayed for a discerning heart. This relates to a wise leader's ability to identify leverage points that will bring about change in the best way possible and to recognize a way forward into the unknown future. It speaks of resourcefulness and competence.

The sound judgment of a leader is often seen in retrospect rather than in the moment. As Jesus reminds us, "Wisdom is justified by all her children" (Luke 7:35). The results of a decided course of action demonstrate whether that decision was a sound judgment. The path is sometimes counterintuitive and countercultural. It takes great courage for a leader to stand for God's ways rather than compromising and aligning with the world's ways.

LEADERS WHO LACK SOUND JUDGMENT

Leaders who fail to exercise sound judgment aim to please people instead of God. They will compromise their convictions or shrink back from taking a stand for fear of falling out of favor or facing strong opposition. They seek to play both sides of the fence, thus neutering their impact and losing credibility. They are the proverbial "weather-vane leader"—whichever way the popularity wind blows, they lead in that direction.

Pontius Pilate was one such leader. When Jesus was brought before him on the initial charge of sedition (a capital crime under Roman law), he determined that Jesus was not guilty. But to please the Jewish accusers, he had Jesus beaten and mocked before them. When this failed to appease them, the charge was changed to apostasy, claiming to be the Son of God. While this was not a capital crime according to Roman law, the governor had discretion in choosing punishments. The Jewish leaders reminded Pilate that Caesar would not look favorably on someone who was leading an insurrection, implying that they would report his not-guilty verdict up the chain of command. Finally, "wishing to satisfy the crowd," Pilate capitulated to their demands and released Jesus to be crucified (Mark 15:1-15).

Recall Peter Senge's proverb, "Today's problems are yesterday's solutions." This insight finds its root in decision-makers who lack sound judgment. Leaders without sound judgment focus on short-term wins, giving little or no thought to the collateral impact from their decisions or the long-term consequences. A lack of sound judgment focuses only on *my problem and its solution* without considering how my solution may affect others. Some consequences are unforeseeable, due to factors beyond our control. But many are foreseeable, and they can be avoided with a little forethought on how today's decision will play itself out in the future.

Lacking sound judgment means we focus on the temporal rather than the eternal. Having sound judgment means knowing that our time on this earth is short and that we will truly find a home in heaven after death. We understand that this world is temporary and that our true destiny is an unseen world yet to come. Thus, we do not live for what is seen, for we know that what is seen will soon disappear and be consumed by what is eternal. We hope in the resurrection of the dead, not the long life of the living. Therefore, we live and lead with an eternal value system, and our decisions reflect these values. Consider the wisdom shown in the leaders on display in Hebrews 11:

> These all died in faith, not having received the things
> promised, but having seen them and greeted them from afar,
> and having acknowledged that they were strangers and exiles
> on the earth. For people who speak thus make it clear that
> they are seeking a homeland. If they had been thinking of
> that land from which they had gone out, they would have had
> opportunity to return. But as it is, they desire a better country,
> that is, a heavenly one. Therefore God is not ashamed to be
> called their God, for he has prepared for them a city.
>
> HEBREWS 11:13-16

Leaders who have sound judgment know that they lead from the inside out; therefore, they will not be tempted to compromise their integrity or go against the Word of God to gain some advantage or solve a problem. Those lacking this quality will justify their actions by the immediacy of the problem, the fact that others are doing it too, or perhaps because it just seems like the right thing to do at the time, regardless of whether or not it contradicts the Word of God. "The end justifies the means," they say. Personally, they say, "Do what I say, not what I do." How devastating to those who are following their example! Situational ethics is shifting sand that can quickly turn into quicksand and ensnare many people. Ground erodes slowly, but small compromises will bring down the house over time, as surely as winter follows autumn. Recall the law of the harvest!

Leaders are seldom satisfied with the status quo; rather, they want to bring change. Ungodly, unwise leaders seek change from selfish motives. (It was a desire for change that inspired Lucifer to lead the cosmic rebellion.) Godly, wise leaders want change that advances God's Kingdom and aligns with His purposes. That change can be motivated by God as His Spirit prompts us to embrace the purposes for which He appointed us to lead. But the world is also prompting us to conform to its ways of doing things. We are exhorted, "Do not conform any longer to the pattern of this world, but be transformed by the renewing of your mind. Then you will be able to test and approve what God's will is—his good, pleasing and perfect will" (Romans 12:2, NIV). The battle rages over the minds and hearts of leaders, demanding our attention and clamoring for submission of our wills.

Let's examine how godly leaders exercise sound judgment in their own lives and leadership.

CHOOSING GOD'S WAYS, NOT MAN'S WAYS

Proverbs 14:12 says, "There is a way that seems right to a man, but its end is the way to death." The world's ways are often logical, common, politically correct, seemingly easier to follow, and may even yield short-term wins. But the world's ways result in long-term loss. In contrast, God's ways are often illogical (counterintuitive from a human perspective) and uncommon. Because so few people choose to follow them, God's ways are countercultural and seemingly difficult to follow. And just because something is uncommon or difficult does not necessarily mean that it must be God's plan. Here again, sound judgment can discern the wise way, not just any way forward.

Leaders with sound judgment differentiate between the ways of the world and the ways of God. They choose to follow the ways of God rather than conform to the normal patterns of the world. Following God's ways requires faith, for faith deals with an unknown future. God's ways for His righteous ones are that we continually live by faith (Romans 1:17) during this life—until we pass through the doorway of death and enter an eternity of walking by sight. He desires dependent children who trust in Him (2 Corinthians 1:8-11), not independent children who trust their own counsel.

Leaders with sound judgment take their counsel from God's Word, seeking to align their lives and leadership around its commands, principles, and promises. They willingly submit themselves to the authority of the Bible and courageously obey it, willing to appear foolish in the eyes of the world to please Christ. Paul reminds us: "God chose the foolish things of the world to shame the wise; God chose the weak things of the world to shame the strong" (1 Corinthians 1:27, NIV). There is risk here, for others may disagree, thinking that the possibility of failure is too great. A wise leader will seek to understand their concerns, address them if possible, and trust God for the outcomes.

Joshua's battle plan for Jericho was to march around the city for seven days and then shout. God's plan for Gideon was to reduce his army from thousands to three hundred. God chose to launch a worldwide movement of the gospel into the nations by investing in a few leaders who were "unschooled, ordinary men" (Acts 4:13, NIV).

God chose to give Paul a thorn in his flesh that he might learn to trust in God's power instead of his own (2 Corinthians 12:7). Through the apostle Paul, God reminds us

> Not many of you were wise according to worldly standards,
> not many were powerful, not many were of noble birth.
> But God chose what is foolish in the world to shame
> the wise; God chose what is weak in the world to shame
> the strong; God chose what is low and despised in the world,
> even things that are not, to bring to nothing things that are,
> so that no human being might boast in the presence of God.
>
> I CORINTHIANS 1:26-29

Wise leaders with sound judgment are humble, for they realize that any success that comes from their leadership is due to God's grace and empowerment, not their own ability.

SEEING THROUGH TO ROOT ISSUES

Sound judgment allows leaders to address seminal issues in ways that result in lasting change for good. When setting direction, leaders with sound judgment anticipate outcomes, seeing obstacles and how to overcome them before starting down the path. Those possessing sound judgment think systemically, realize that one course of action may impact other arenas, and prepare for these possible consequences ahead of time.

Things are not always as they appear; therefore, a leader who exercises sound judgment will not assume that what appears to be true now concludes a matter. More data can cause our conclusions to change. With the addition of more information, what we thought was so obvious can now appear to be just the opposite. The foolish rush ahead with decisions based on incomplete data. Good decision-making is knowing when one has enough information to decide. Be decisive, but also, be wise!

I was leading my first team meeting with a group of key student leaders for our campus ministry in Indonesia. My Western, individualistic mind-set and a desire for efficiency propelled me to select a few key people to help plan the semester activities. That was the way I had learned to lead a planning meeting as we sought to organize the semester's goals and activities.

As I extended the invitations and explained my intentions to just a few influential students, I began to get some immediate feedback. "Tom, you cannot have this meeting with just us. We must also include this person and that person. And if they come, then we must also invite so-and-so." My small, efficient planning meeting was suddenly growing into a major event. Instead of a planning team that consisted of four students, we now had thirty-six people around the room. What would have taken half a day to plan now took three days. I reluctantly agreed to their wisdom but told myself that when these students grew to maturity, they would understand that efficiency demands a smaller team.

Surprisingly, it was I who changed instead of them. I came to realize that my priorities were not appropriate to the context of Indonesia. The culture is group oriented and highly inclusive. Their worldview is event oriented, not focused on hours, minutes, or seconds. I grew to see the beauty of having many people speak into plans that we made. Yes, it took three days to plan a semester, but the amount of time taken was not as important as the process we used. We made our plans, but we did it in a different way. Ownership was created as many people shaped the goals and activities, and many grew as we wrestled with the implications of our plans. In this area, it turned out, it was I who needed the maturity, not them.

Leaders with sound judgment also recognize the spiritual component to our Kingdom leadership. We are being actively opposed by an unseen world of evil spirits. We would be foolish to not recognize that our enemy deploys evil forces to frustrate our efforts. "For our struggle is not against flesh and blood, but against the rulers, against the authorities, against the powers of this dark world and against the spiritual forces of evil in the heavenly realms" (Ephesians 6:12, NIV). While not every problem we encounter finds its origin in the devil, we must not be ignorant of this reality either. Good judgment means waging spiritual warfare while clothed with the armor of God. We must pray against the forces of evil and fight the spiritual fight with the armor God provides (Ephesians 6:10-17). When things don't make sense or just seem weird, we are wise to assume that the evil one is active in the situation and act accordingly.

CHOOSING BETWEEN GOOD, BETTER, AND BEST

Choosing between good and bad options is easy. But when we must select between options that are all seemingly good, how do we choose? Strategic leadership means that we know our mission, vision, and outcomes, as well as our strategy for accomplishing them. It seems that there are always more opportunities than resources to meet them. Thus, the need arises for choosing where to allocate people and money to achieve the best outcomes.

Sound judgment allows leaders to determine the path to the best *return on investment* in the strategic deployment of limited resources. Jesus demonstrated this when He chose to concentrate on the development of twelve disciples instead of a broad teaching and healing ministry. He realized that the world-changing move-ment that He was launching needed well-trained leadership; thus, He selected twelve leaders to train during the final two years of His public ministry (Mark 3:14). These leaders would be the leverage needed to ensure the founding and growth of the church.

When I was leading The Navigators' Collegiate ministry, we

frequently had to determine which new campuses to select for launching new ministries. What criteria would we use? Should we add staff to a current team or launch a new ministry on a different campus? Would it be wise to choose the campuses with the most students? Certainly, that can be a consideration, for a campus with fifty thousand students seems to present more opportunity for ministry than campuses with five thousand. But how many students can a staff team truly impact? It seems that every team has a finite capacity, regardless of the number of students around them. Would it be better to influence an entire small campus or make a relatively smaller impact on a much larger one? Would it be best to focus on dorm residents or the Greek system? Urban campuses or rural? And what about community colleges with two-year students as opposed to state universities with four-year students? How should we factor into our decision the fact that other student ministries were already operating on a campus? All these considerations, and many more, made sound judgment paramount when choosing where to place new staff teams among many potential campuses.

Our strategy led us to leave unstaffed those campuses where our teams could not be well cared for. Because we did not have adequate leadership capacity in the Pacific Northwest, for example, we chose to multistaff and pioneer new campus ministries in other US regions where we had leaders already in place. The Pacific Northwest would have to wait until we had a leader in place. We prioritized providing our staff with good leadership and supervision.

We had not planned to open a work at Boston University in the near future. But then a plea from a faculty member, who offered to sponsor us on the campus, led to adjusting our timeline. We saw it as a "Macedonian call" similar to the one Paul received in Troas (Acts 16:9-10).

Because the Great Commission (Matthew 28:18-20) calls us to make disciples of all the people of the world, The Navigators are committed to reaching and discipling people not just in America but also throughout the whole world. Requests for US staff to serve as cross-cultural missionaries in various countries are taken very seriously. Besides the cross-cultural competency of the individual staff, one major factor in those decisions is the host country's ability to supervise and care for these missionaries. That has led us to say "no, not at this time" to many needy situations as we kept in tension what was best for the mission and what was best for its people.

Sound judgment allows leaders to sort through multiple options and discern what choice is best for a time and place. Sound judgment means wading through emotions and the cacophony of different voices to know God's way forward.

Wise Kingdom leaders learn to listen to the voice of the Spirit within them as they sort through various options. When confused or uncertain, they pray for insight and guidance. Isaiah says, "Your ears shall hear a word behind you, saying, 'This is the way, walk in it'" (Isaiah 30:21). Our spirits will hear His Spirit directing us, always in alignment with His Word, and we will know His best path. I often remind others that knowing the will of God is not that difficult. God speaks very clearly. It's *obeying the voice of God once we hear it* that is the real challenge!

JUDGMENT IN PROBLEM-SOLVING

Leaders are problem-solvers. Sound judgment allows leaders to make the complex simple and help make the difficult easy. With it, leaders can also address short- and long-term solutions to complex issues and remove obstacles from the pathway toward progress in our mission.

Learning to make the complexities of life and leadership simple is part of sound judgment. Avoiding oversimplification also relates to godly wisdom. Einstein said, "Everything should be made as simple as possible, but not simpler." He simplified quantum physics into a very simple equation: $E = mc^2$. Now, I don't begin to pretend to understand the complexity behind this equation, but I admire his ability to simplify complexity.

There is a difference between *simple* and *simplistic*. In our desire for simplicity, we sometimes so reduce the issue that we neglect or overlook some key components. This overly reductionist approach yields solutions that won't work or won't stand the test of time. We may find short-term solutions only to realize later that we created unintended, problematic consequences.

Leaders are often involved in complexities beyond their experience. The easy issues are solved before they come to you. It is usually the truly difficult, messy issue that gets passed along until it arrives at your inbox. I'm often confronted with problems that I have no idea how to even begin to solve. Added pressure comes from others having tried obvious solutions that have not led to a final resolution of the issue. What to do?

When facing a situation like this, one habit that I've learned is to simply bow my heart before the Lord and confess my lack of wisdom, experience, ideas, or resources to solve the issue. I cry out to Him in prayer with a simple "Lord, help me." I remind Him of His promise to deliver me in times of trouble when I ask Him for help (Psalm 50:15). And He always shows me a way forward. It may not be the complete answer to my dilemma, but it is a step forward. And then, when that step is completed, He shows me that next step, and so forth, until the problem is behind me and I'm on to the next one.

Sound judgment allows Kingdom leaders to bring clarity from confusion and maintain focus on the mission without getting distracted by multiple opportunities. The Spirit of God can bring illumination to truth and creativity to problem-solving as we lead.

DEVOTIONAL REFLECTION

BIBLE REFLECTION

Read and reflect on the following passages regarding sound judgment. Note particularly the applications to life situations.

- 1 Samuel 16:7

- Proverbs 13:20

- Romans 16:19

PRAYER ITEMS

- Ask God to teach you how to exercise sound judgment in problem-solving.

- Ask the Lord to give you faith and courage to face the pressure of conforming to the world and the current cultural tide.

PERSONAL APPLICATIONS

- List some of the major questions or challenges that you are facing in this current season of life. Create a minimum of three answers or solutions to each, and then discuss the possible long-term consequences of each with your spouse, close friend, or team. Look for the one best solution together.

- Study the book of Ecclesiastes and note what is deemed vain and temporal by nature and contrast that with what is considered eternal and worthy of our life focus. Look for personal applications from this study.

7

UNDERSTANDING

I, wisdom, dwell together with prudence;
I possess knowledge and discretion.
To fear the LORD *is to hate evil;*
I hate pride and arrogance,
evil behavior and perverse speech.
Counsel and sound judgment are mine;
I have **understanding** *and power.*

PROVERBS 8:12-14, NIV

I am disturbed when I see the majority of so-called Christians having
such little understanding of the real nature of the faith they profess.
Faith is a subject of such importance that we should not ignore it
because of the distractions or the hectic pace of our lives.

WILLIAM WILBERFORCE

UNDERSTANDING IS THE ABILITY to see the relationships between a series of facts. As such, it is closely related to knowledge. Once we have gathered knowledge, this information must be correlated in our minds so we can understand how things work or how they influence each other. The world uses the scientific method to show the relationship of various elements. Once an experiment is shown to be repeatable, we arrive at a certain level of understanding. For example, when we apply heat to water, we know that the water boils when it reaches 212°F (100°C) at sea level. By combining the facts we know about water and heat, we understand that by turning on a stove and applying heat to the bottom of a pan of water, it will boil at a very specific temperature, given enough heat and time. This type of understanding is useful in life, but it is still short of the goal of wisdom.

Understanding in the Kingdom sense has to do with the "God-given perception of the nature and meaning of things . . . the ability to discern spiritual truth and to apply it to human disposition and conduct."[1] It is the ability to know how to use the knowledge one possesses.[2]

Understanding allows us to discern trends or patterns in behavior, seeing whether something is a onetime aberration or the beginning of something new. Understanding patterns of behavior helps us to not only see actions but also discern motivations. Additionally, it helps us see a person's strengths for contribution and then position them where they can contribute from these strengths. It allows a leader to select and recruit valuable team members who are complementary in their strengths to yield a well-balanced team.

Understanding that leads to godly wisdom sees interconnectedness and repeating patterns, sequences, or progressions with predictable outcomes. Moses, for example, knew the ways that God interacted with His people and thus could align his leadership with the Lord's character and purposes. Contrast that with the lack of understanding sometimes exhibited by Jesus' disciples. Shortly after Jesus miraculously fed four thousand people, He and His disciples entered a boat to go to the other side of the Sea of Galilee (see Matthew 16:5-12). Along the way, Jesus exhorted the Twelve to "Be on your guard against the yeast of the Pharisees and Sadducees" (NIV). They immediately concluded that it was because they had forgotten to take enough bread along for their journey. When Jesus reminded them of the recent miraculous provision of bread (and fish) to thousands of people, they accurately recounted the events, even the amount of leftovers. They had good knowledge! But they still did not have understanding. Eventually, with Jesus' help, the Twelve came to realize that the "yeast" Jesus was talking about referred to teachings of the Pharisees and Sadducees, which they were to avoid. The disciples moved from knowledge to understanding as they thought more deeply about their recent experiences.

Understanding that leads to godly wisdom includes what we can observe about God's character manifesting itself in the way He interacts with people in the Bible. For example, we will realize that God makes promises, and that because of His very nature, He does not lie or change. Therefore, we understand that His promises found in Scripture can be trusted. Psalm 119:140 says, "Your promises have been thoroughly tested, and your servant loves them" (NIV). Our love for God's promises (and the Promiser) will grow as we prove the promises true by seeing them fulfilled in life.

Growing in spiritual understanding means that we will also begin seeing repeating patterns in the Scriptures. For example, we begin by knowing that God is outside of time and that "with the Lord a day is as a thousand years, and a thousand years as one day" (2 Peter 3:8). We observe that Noah spent one hundred years building the ark before the first raindrop fell. We see that God's promise of a son to Abraham and Sarah took twenty-five years to complete. And the promised return of Christ has taken over two millennia, and we continue to wait. This knowledge helps us understand that God's timing is not always our timing; in fact, His timetable is often longer than our own. But people with this understanding also know that God's timing is always perfect.

LEADERS WHO LACK UNDERSTANDING

People without godly understanding don't see the relationship between personal time with God and their leadership. They don't pursue a growing relationship with God by spending time with Him in prayer and in His Word. They are so busy doing *for* the King that they neglect time *with* the King. The result is a lack of understanding His ways and truths that would help in discerning root issues or identifying best choices for solving life's problems.

Leaders who lack understanding tend to repeat their mistakes. They never seem to find the time to stop and reflect on their previous experience, asking God to teach them what they need to learn from it. They fail to connect previous experience to their current situation and thus must continually relearn lessons.

These unwise leaders lack understanding when selecting team members. They select people based on external qualities (competency-based selection) only, instead of also considering internal qualities. External qualities are the measurables—what we put in our résumé. While competency is important, it must also be paired with internal qualities (like character, work style, and attitude) to determine best fit and whether one will function well on a team. Discerning these internal qualities, especially in a short interview, is an art form to develop.

Leaders struggle to maintain a cohesive team when they are unable to position people according to complementary strengths. And in their lack of emotional intelligence, they fail to build a team that works with synergy, where the sum is greater than the individual parts. Instead, they coordinate a swim team of individual performances and miss a great opportunity for the multiplying impact of complementary, synergistic teamwork. Their teams are frequently dysfunctional, with team members outwardly complying but inwardly pursuing their own individualistic ends. They give lip service to agreed-upon team goals but are not committed to the success of the whole team, only to their individual part.

These people fail to understand that life is a marathon, not a dash. They do not consider their God-given capacities or accept their limitations; they frequently exceed their boundaries, living without margin and leading from depleted personal resources rather than from an overflow. They fail to run life at a rhythm that is sustainable long-term and frequently need extended breaks to replenish, only to find themselves quickly depleted again. They don't see the importance of getting regular adequate rest and exercise, eating wisely, or attending to daily spiritual disciplines. Oh yes, they may intellectually assent to these things and even practice them off and on, but they are not convinced of their importance, for they soon slip back into their old ways and wonder why they lack energy and zeal. Worse yet, they justify their poor choices by blaming their God-given design, circumstances, genetics, or the devil, when they are not victims but willing participants. Our behaviors are born from our beliefs and convictions; thus, we choose to act out of what we believe, and these choices are both revealing and convicting.

Let's examine how wise leaders exercise understanding in their own lives and leadership.

UNDERSTANDING GOD'S WAYS

One of God's ways is that He begins with something small and grows it incrementally bigger. We see this illustrated in the parable of the mustard seed (Matthew 13:31-32) and the parable of the yeast (Matthew 13:33). Understanding leaders know that lasting impact and influence is built over time. They realize that God's timetable is often longer than they are comfortable with or think necessary.

Consequently, wise leaders are not impatient. Keeping in step with God's ways, understanding leaders don't neglect laying solid foundations and support structures that will sustain a long-term endeavor. They don't give in to the temptation to appear cutting edge; rather, they opt for God's proven way. This is not to imply that they are risk averse, but that they are wise in deciding which risks to expose themselves to. A leader who exercises understanding can discern between what is popular and trendy versus what is eternal and lasting. They seek to align themselves with God's ways in their personal lifestyle choices and in their leadership styles.

Another of God's ways is to act locally but see globally—being aware of the larger context of our actions. The entire world, all the nations (peoples) of the world, are within God's scope and plan; therefore, our local actions must align with His bigger purposes. Understanding leaders lead locally but constantly lift their gaze to the horizon, knowing that the whole world is on God's heart.

Understanding leaders focus on the internal, not the just the external, for they know that it is from the heart of a man that both good things and bad things come (Mark 7:20-23). The religious leaders of Jesus' time were externally focused. They sought "success" in being ceremonially clean and righteous, but in their hearts, they were unclean.

Paul could distinguish between external and eternal righteousness.

If anyone else thinks he has reason for confidence in the flesh, I have more: circumcised on the eighth day, of the people of Israel, of the tribe of Benjamin, a Hebrew of Hebrews; as to the law, a Pharisee; as to zeal, a persecutor of the church; as to righteousness under the law, blameless. But whatever gain I had, I counted as loss for the sake of Christ. Indeed, I count everything as loss because of the surpassing worth of knowing Christ Jesus my Lord. For his sake I have suffered the loss of all things and count them as rubbish, in order that I may gain Christ and be found in him, not having a righteousness of my own that comes from the law, but that which comes through faith in Christ, the righteousness from God that depends on faith.

PHILIPPIANS 3:4-9

People with godly understanding will not neglect the internal as they seek to accomplish their mission. That concern extends to those they are leading. As they care for and develop those they lead, they seek to bring heart-level change.

One can get short-term, superficial change by focusing on external behavioral change. This will only last until the reinforcing environment changes. Lasting behavioral change results from changes in one's heart and mind. It is in our beliefs that behaviors are birthed and lasting change begins. These beliefs result in new values, which in turn lead to new choices, and then ultimately, new behavior that will abide.

LeRoy Eims, former foundational leader of The Navigators, often said, "There are two ways to miss the will of God—sin and glorious opportunities." An understanding leader keeps this in mind! I remember when the Super Bowl was being broadcast by satellite in Indonesia for the first time in history. I was asked to be the color commentator for the national broadcast that would touch millions. (Before you think too highly of me, know that the list of people who were fluent in the language and knew the rules of the game was very short.) The offer was particularly tempting because it paid a healthy onetime fee. As I thought and prayed about this opportunity, however, God helped me realize the short-term distraction it would be for our local ministry and the potential long-term distraction it would be if this exposure lead to other opportunities. It did not align with why we left home and traveled halfway around the world. Short-term look, very interesting. Long-term look, not helpful or beneficial. I said no with an overwhelming sense of peace that it was the right choice.

Wise, understanding leaders aim for long-term impact, not short-term wins. While short-term wins are good for overcoming inertia and gaining momentum, they are not our aim. God's timetable is long-term. Wise leaders with understanding aim for the ripple impact of their leadership, not the splash!

UNDERSTANDING GOD'S TRUTHS AND OUR TIMES

The Word of God is the good seed that springs to life in the hearts of individuals, bringing them from darkness to life (see the parable of the sower in Mark 4). It is the Word of God that the Holy Spirit uses to bring forth new life (1 Peter 1:23). Therefore, understanding leaders seek to lead from the Scriptures and into the Scriptures, for they know that it is God's Word that is used to change people from the inside out. We start by understanding the principles of the Kingdom and leadership found in the Bible. Then, we lead into the Scriptures by applying the Bible to our leadership context for answers to life's issues.

Wisely applying God's truth also requires an understanding of our context. We must be able to observe the circumstance, consider the Scriptures and how they intersect with it, and integrate the Scriptures into our response. We must strive to be like the men of Issachar who came to help David, who "understood the times and knew what Israel should do" (1 Chronicles 12:32, NIV).

Understanding leaders know that the gospel message can be clouded or confusing when combined with additional cultural baggage. They focus on the purity of the gospel, seeking to contextualize approaches in ministry that keep a clear focus on Him and not methodology or traditions. They remember Paul's comments:

> To the Jews I became as a Jew, in order to win Jews. To those under the law I became as one under the law (though not being myself under the law) that I might win those under the law. To those outside the law I became as one outside the law (not being outside the law of God but under the law of Christ) that I might win those outside the law. To the weak I became weak, that I might win the weak. I have become all things to all people, that by all means I might save some.
>
> I CORINTHIANS 9:20-22

Jesus is the perfect example of an understanding leader. "Jesus . . . was able to communicate to people completely on terms which were understandable to them."[3] He took upon Himself the form of a man and lived the life of a Jewish rabbi. "He willingly submitted to certain restrictions and yet overcame them to accomplish his mission."[4]

Although Jesus adapted Himself to the audience He was seeking to reach, He sometimes deliberately violated the cultural practices of the day. Kingdom values took precedent, and He willingly accepted opposition, scorn, and misunderstanding out of fidelity to the Kingdom.

Let's note a few of the examples where Jesus did *not* follow the Jewish cultural norms of His day.

- Jesus talked to a Samaritan woman (John 4:1-27). It was not culturally appropriate for Jesus, a Jewish rabbi, to talk to a woman, especially since she was a Samaritan, for the Jews disliked the Samaritans very much.[5]

- Jesus and His disciples did not fast (Mark 2:18-22). It was the practice of devout Jews to fast regularly. (The Pharisees fasted twice a week.)

- Jesus did not do the ceremonial washings before eating (see, for example, Mark 7:1-8). The Pharisees would go through a series of washings before eating to remove any defilement from entering their body.

- Jesus touched lepers and the dead (Mark 1:40-42; 5:41; Luke 8:51-56). Lepers were considered unclean, and having contact with them was considered most defiling. Dead bodies were also considered a source of defilement for Jews.

- Jesus associated with the unclean and culturally marginalized (Luke 5:29-32; 7:36-50; 19:1-10). Prostitutes, tax collectors, and the like were considered sinners and were to be avoided as sources of defilement.[6]

Yet for all His willingness to violate cultural norms, Jesus was also culturally accommodating at times. Below are some examples of when Jesus *did* follow the norms of the day.

- Jesus went to the synagogue to worship on the Sabbath (Luke 4:16). Synagogue worship started during Babylonian captivity, after the Temple was destroyed and the Jews were removed from Palestine. It continued after the rebuilding of the Temple and the return of the Jews to the Promised Land.

- Jesus celebrated the Jewish festivals, even those that were not prescribed in the Old Testament, such as the Feast of Dedication (John 10:22-23). The Feast of Dedication was initiated during the intertestamental period and is not prescribed in the Old Testament law. The feast (Hanukkah) "commemorated the purifying of the temple, the removal of the old polluted altar, and the restoration of the worship of Jehovah by Judas Maccabeus, BC 164."[7]

- Jesus paid the Temple tax (Matthew 17:24-27). The Temple tax was reinstituted by Nehemiah after the captivity at one-third of a shekel, but the tax rate used during Jesus' time was the rate originally prescribed by Moses (cf. Exodus 30:11-16 and Nehemiah 10:32).[8]

Understanding leaders pursue increasing depth in the Scriptures and discernment of the cultural norms of their day. They seek wisdom in applying the Scriptures to their leadership context, comparing and contrasting what is culturally accepted with the truth of God's Word. Issues such as suicide, euthanasia, sexuality and sexual identity, aging, retirement, racism, and immigration are but a few of the pressing topics screaming for biblical guidance and wise leadership.

A guiding principle would seem to be this: We should strive to make Jesus and the Bible the only basis of our ministry and the only stumbling block if the message is to be rejected. In instances where Kingdom values or practices violate the local cultural norms or procedures, we must hold fast to biblical truth and accept the resulting opposition from the culture. This does not mean we should flaunt our convictions, especially if we know they are likely to cause adverse reactions. We must be sensitive as we take our stand, so that the opposition we face is an opposition to Christ and not to insensitivity or cultural blind spots. This is an opportunity to see God demonstrate His power and grace despite cultural barriers.

UNDERSTANDING PEOPLE

God has hardwired into the hearts and minds of people their personal temperaments. These temperaments are modified and weaknesses are changed over time through spiritual maturity and the filling of His Spirit in our lives. But our basic temperaments do not change. They are a God-given baseline from which we view the world and interact with others. Wise leaders seek to understand their own temperament and the temperaments of each of those they labor with, knowing their strengths and weaknesses to better serve them. We must be careful not to label others by their temperament and remember that all of us are growing toward spiritual maturity. Jesus again becomes our model. It is seemingly impossible to label Him with a singular temperament type, for His is perfectly mature.

An understanding leader will seek to populate a leadership team with people of complementary gifting and strengths. The mantra "Operate in your strengths and staff to your weaknesses" is a truism worth remembering. If teammates are given responsibilities in line with their gifting, then they will be highly motivated and their leadership influence will be great.

Much of Kingdom leadership is learning to work well with others. Having high emotional intelligence enables leaders to accomplish much with others. These leaders understand their own emotional state and that of those they interact with. They recognize and honor generational, gender, positional, cultural, and ethnic differences, and then adapt their leadership to their audience for maximum impact.

UNDERSTANDING OURSELVES

We will want to understand our own temperament, as well as our spiritual gifts, natural abilities, and individual capacities. All of these affect our leadership—not only determining how we lead but also what type of leadership best fits us. Some people are designed for more direct leadership responsibilities—banding a local team together to accomplish a mission. And others are better designed for indirect leadership contributions—organizing large groups of geographically dispersed, local teams, setting direction and aligning resources to accomplish a larger mission.

Some of us are more naturally self-aware and sensitive to the emotional state of ourselves and others. For those of us (me included) who are not designed this way, we can learn and grow in this area. When asked, "How do you feel?" my answer frequently can be summed up in "I'm happy," "I'm sad," or "I'm frustrated." That limited emotional vocabulary is not conducive to in-depth, heart-to-heart conversations with others, especially my wife! So I've had to try to expand my emotional vocabulary, asking God to make me more aware of my own emotions and help me express them well. It is then that I'm able to recognize the emotions of others and align my leadership in such a way as to best serve them. While emotional intelligence may never be a strength, we can avoid it being a crippling weakness that hinders us from leading well.

UNDERSTANDING GOD'S TIMETABLE

Wise, understanding leaders seek to create a pace and rhythm to life that is sustainable over long time frames. Paul reminds us that life is a uniquely individualized race that we are called to run hard to the finish line (see 1 Corinthians 9:24-27; Philippians 3:12-14; Hebrews 12:1-2). It's a long race with many twists and turns. In their zeal and inexperience, youth often fail to see the need to pace themselves for the long race, and thus they fall by the wayside, failing to finish what they so grandly began.

Understanding leaders recognize the difference between life's pace and rhythm. Pace is how fast we are going at a particular moment. Rhythm is pace stretched out over a long time or season. Pace varies from high RPMs to low, depending on the season and context. There are times when we must run at a very high pace to meet the demands on us. But these times have a beginning and an end. Understanding leaders know that this redline pace cannot be sustained long-term without suffering serious consequences to physical, emotional, and spiritual heath, family relationships, or job performance. Thus, they are willing to engage in a frenetic pace only when keeping an end in sight. They ensure that periods of intensity are followed by slower-pace times for rebuilding reserve and preparing for their next redline pace. In this way, they avoid burnout or a desperate need for a long break from responsibility. The fool says, "Better to flame out than rust out." The wise, understanding leader says, "Run hard to the finish line. But run with wisdom and perseverance, for it is a very long race."

We are to give this type of all-out commitment and effort, with wisdom and perseverance, when running our own race of faithfulness. Paul puts it this way:

Do you not know that in a race all the runners run, but
only one receives the prize? So run that you may obtain it.
Every athlete exercises self-control in all things. They do it
to receive a perishable wreath, but we an imperishable. So
I do not run aimlessly; I do not box as one beating the air.
But I discipline my body and keep it under control, lest after
preaching to others I myself should be disqualified.

I CORINTHIANS 9:24-27

Run in such a way as to get the prize. That means giving yourself
fully to the race, but it also means keeping the true finish line in view.
Our times demand understanding leaders who have the wisdom to
navigate the complexities of modern life and culture without compromising the truth of the Kingdom—to run with perseverance and
understanding.

DEVOTIONAL REFLECTION

BIBLE REFLECTION

Read and reflect on the following passages regarding the wise use of understanding. Note particularly the applications to life situations.

- Psalm 119:97-100

- Proverbs 3:5-6

- Colossians 1:9-10

PRAYER ITEMS

- Ask God to help you grow in emotional intelligence, becoming more aware of your own emotional state and the emotional states of those around you. Ask Him to help you understand how to better express those emotions to others.

- Ask God to teach you His ways, just as He did with Moses (see Exodus 33:12-23).

PERSONAL APPLICATIONS

- Reflect on the amount of time you spend in God's Word and in prayer. Are you getting enough input from Him to live and lead from an overflow? What does He want you to do differently?

- Reflect on your life's current pace and long-term rhythm. Does your current pace reflect a sustainable rhythm that will allow you to run long with perseverance and finish well? What does He want you to do about any changes needed?

8

POWER

I, wisdom, dwell together with prudence;
I possess knowledge and discretion.
To fear the LORD is to hate evil;
I hate pride and arrogance,
evil behavior and perverse speech.
Counsel and sound judgment are mine;
*I have understanding and **power**.*

PROVERBS 8:12-14, NIV

Nearly all men can stand adversity, but if you want
to test a man's character, give him power.

ABRAHAM LINCOLN

WE NOW CONCLUDE our focus on the four applications of wisdom in the life of a leader: counsel, sound judgment, understanding, and power. The final application is power.

By *power* we mean the ability to act, to produce an effect. Power involves having authority over others and possessing qualities that allow individuals to achieve their aims. Within godly leaders, this power is often seen as an inner strength—personal courage to trust God to accomplish what that leader has determined as their divine purpose. Wise leaders seek to use both positional and personal authority to serve and bless others. Positional authority comes with the organizational title or job and is defined by one's job description. Personal authority is authority voluntarily given by another to you based upon your character or perceived competency and is not limited by any role or responsibility. Wise leaders do not use either type of authority to promote themselves or further selfish ambition. They know that to have institutional power is not necessarily to have Kingdom power, and to have Kingdom power is not necessarily to have institutional power.

LEADERS WHO LACK GODLY POWER

Unwise leaders fail to effectively use the positional power that comes with their leadership roles. They don't recognize that their words can wound others; thus, their criticism outweighs their affirmation and their words continue scarring others long after they were said. They insensitively neglect (and sometimes refuse) to affirm others, falsely fearing that it may breed a proud spirit. They can fail to praise others for a job well done because successfully completing the job was expected. This critical attitude makes them difficult to work with. In a volunteer environment, the volunteers "vote with their feet" and leave.

Unwise leaders do not understand the power of their personal example. They fail to notice that others are watching and imitating them. And they are often surprised when teammates leave, accusing those leaving of disloyalty after having been chosen to be on their leadership team in the first place.

Lacking God's power, these leaders tend to rely on their own abilities. They micromanage others, and this spirit of control gives them a false sense of importance. All things must be inspected and signed off on by them. They become the organizational bottleneck as decisions await their approval. They don't readily give authority to others or empower them to accomplish a mission; rather, they jealously guard their power, keeping it instead of sharing it.

Unwise leaders don't share credit—or worse yet, they take credit for someone else's accomplishments. They don't share the spotlight with others, and because of their own insecurities, they would not think of championing another. They think, *If I promote this person, they are so talented that they may one day take my job.* They are not generous in word or deed, and they desperately cling to their position. If asked to transition their role to another, instead of setting the new person up for success, they seek to keep institutional power, because the position is their sole source of power and identity. But wise, godly leaders are givers, not takers!

Unwise leaders don't give others a second chance. They create a "one strike and you're out" environment. Perfectionism is mistaken for excellence, and anything less than perfect is deemed a failure. Those who don't measure up to this unrealistic standard are rejected and replaced by a new person. Developing others is not part of their view of leadership; thus, they keep looking for perfect people and wonder why they can't find them.

POWER AND AUTHORITY

All power and authority find their source in the relational dynamic of leader and follower. Note what the devil offers Jesus in the second desert temptation: "The devil led him up to a high place and showed him in an instant all the kingdoms of the world. And he said to him, "I will give you all their authority and splendor, for it has been given to me, and I can give it to anyone I want to" (Luke 4:5-6, NIV). Jesus would have to first acknowledge the devil's leadership, then be given worldly power. Jesus did not refute the devil's ability to give it. The devil has authority, but it is limited under the ultimate authority of Christ, who has "all authority in heaven and on earth" (Matthew 28:18).

Contrasted with worldly power founded on a leader-follower relationship is the power that comes from the Lord—an anointing of His Spirit that is given to accomplish His purposes in and through us. Through the blood of Christ and because of His atonement, believers now have power over sin, demons, and our ultimate enemy, death. God's servant leaders are given authority to lead and influence others and are called to steward that influence well. Spiritual leaders will all give an account to Him of how they use this authority and influence (see Hebrews 13:17).

With positional leadership comes a certain amount of authority to set direction, distribute resources, and solve missional challenges. It is a privilege and a sobering responsibility to have positional authority. But positional authority is limited by one's rank or title. Kingdom leaders do not have carte blanche to rule by fiat! They, too, are leaders under authority.

If you poll emerging leaders from the Millennial generation and ask them how they perceive the subject of authority, their response is overwhelmingly negative. In fact, in a recent meeting, one young person said, "I'm trying to learn how to lead without using authority." Well, good luck with that one!

This person's intent was to use authority in an unoppressive or unharmful way. In that person's experience, all those in authority had either greatly disappointed or taken advantage of them. Parents had divorced each other, trusted family members had abused them, and teachers or religious leaders had used their position for their own ends. In this case, it is understandable why power and authority are viewed with such a negative perspective.

But there is a second type of authority and power that has far greater ability to influence people—personal authority. For Kingdom leaders, personal authority is built as trust grows between the leader and those being led. It arises from the leader's growing intimacy with God. That relationship is recognized by others, and they willingly give the leader power to influence them, trusting that God is speaking to and guiding the leader. This voluntary submission to another's influence allows a leader to speak to heart issues, character issues, and areas that are outside of the mission or task. A wise leader will not assume this authority but will always ask permission to speak into these areas before addressing them.

Leaders can grow in their ability to influence others as they gain more experience. You've seen this before and know what to expect, and therefore your confidence regarding how to handle this situation breeds confidence in others.

POWER AND COMPETENCY

Power and influence can be gained through increased competency. A trained, skilled leader will find that others willingly follow them because they believe they are being led by someone who knows what to do. For Kingdom leaders, in addition to growing in leadership skills, a growing competency in applying the Bible to life and leadership adds to their personal authority (see 2 Timothy 2:15).

We must also acknowledge that certain personalities seem to influence others more naturally. Those who are more extroverted in their personality type, more people oriented, would have more of a penchant for influencing the tone and culture of a larger group. This natural ability to influence is enhanced through spiritual gifting and the Spirit's empowerment. But does God only use extroverts to lead on a larger scale? While introverts can be good at gaining trust and building loyalty with individuals, can God use introverts to lead broadly? After all, they are 50 percent of the human race!

Some years ago, I read a biography of D. L. Moody. The book related an incident in Moody's life where he did not sense God's power when he preached. He desired to see God use him in greater ways to influence people through his public ministry of the Word. Moody began to pray for greater power when he preached God's Word. He asked God for a special anointing to move the hearts of people as he proclaimed the gospel to the lost. God answered Moody's prayer, resulting in a much greater response to his public ministry.[1]

As I've followed Moody's example, that passage has become a personal promise for my own public ministry of God's Word. Because my God-given temperament makes me more of an introvert, I find comfort in people like Saul, who were hesitant to assume the role of leader. Saul was probably introverted (or at least shy); he was hiding when the selection council met at Mizpah to choose their first king (1 Samuel 10:17-24).

I began to pray over 1 Samuel 10:6 regularly before I spoke publicly, saying something like this:

Lord, just as you promised through Samuel to Saul that your Spirit would enable him to proclaim your truth with power and change him into a different person, I'm asking that you do that for me. May these people hear you speaking through me as you make me into your spokesman. May my words be empowered by you to touch their hearts as well as their heads. And may lasting change come about because of this speaking opportunity.

This prayer pattern has become my habit every time I have the privilege to stand before people and share His Word. And I, too, sense, like Moody, that it has truly made a difference in my public ministry.

Wise leaders know that they exercise power and that this power can build up or tear down. It can be used for blessing or damaging others. And they are aware that they will one day be held accountable to God for the use of their leadership power. Thus, they are circumspect in its use and loving in its exercise.

Let's examine how good leaders exercise power wisely in their own lives and leadership.

THE POWER OF WORDS

One of the initial observations I made when I accepted an organizational leadership role was that my words were frequently quoted by those around me. Before I assumed a leadership role, my words were not often remembered. But after I became a leader, things changed.

I would be interacting with someone, and they would say, "Tom, when we spoke a year ago, you said . . ." I was shocked that they remembered; I did not even recall the conversation, let alone what I had said. I hadn't changed over the previous year, but my role had. I quickly learned to be more circumspect in my public opinions and that there were certain subjects where my thoughts were best kept to myself. And when I did share an opinion, I needed to lead with a disclaimer like "Well, this is what I think at this moment. But my thoughts aren't completely formed yet, so please don't take them as final."

The power of words can be used for great blessing. By genuinely affirming another for a job well done, you can mark them deeply, and they will remember your words when facing future challenging times. Your affirmation will validate the growing sense that they can do what they've been asked to do and that they are doing a job well. And your words will motivate and inspire them to keep going when things don't work out the way they had intended.

We must differentiate between affirmation and flattery. *Flattery* is praising another for something that they had no control over. For example, "You have beautiful eyes" can be flattery if said from a desire to manipulate rather than as a heartfelt expression of love, as the person has no control over the shape, color, or positioning of their eyes. They were born that way! Those who flatter often want to praise with the desire to control. Don't flatter others; affirm them!

I've made it a habit to affirm others when I see them doing a good job. There are so few people in my own life who genuinely affirm me that it sometimes appears that the entire world is full of my critics. Those who affirm me are very rare, and their words are like water in a desert.

Wise leaders know that their words carry influence in others' lives. They think before they speak, and they sometimes choose not to express their thoughts because they don't want to be quoted later. They also know that their criticism of others can wound people deeply; therefore, they choose their words carefully when giving developmental feedback. And they also regularly practice verbal affirmation for a job well done, knowing that this breeds confidence and joy in those who hear it.

Not long ago, I was in a restaurant waiting for my lunch appointment to arrive. While sitting at my table, I noticed a waitress meticulously cleaning and setting the table next to me. Her excellence and attention to detail were evident in this seemingly mundane task. I saw an opportunity for affirmation.

I called her over and simply stated that she was representing her company very well by her attention to detail. As a customer who came to this establishment regularly, I really appreciated her thoughtfulness.

What happened next surprised me. Tears welled up in her eyes and she said that yes, she did strive for excellence in every detail of her job, even down to setting the table with outstanding quality. She expressed gratefulness that someone noticed, and thanked me for sharing that with her. Imagine what that brief interaction would have been like if it had been her supervisor who had said those things to her! I have seen similar reactions from others who are in service jobs where they interact with the general public. The only time they hear from their customers is when something is wrong, and we often have bad attitudes, demanding that they do something immediately to right a wrong. How refreshing to speak words of affirmation. The shock value alone will make someone's day!

THE POWER OF EXAMPLE

Leaders are always setting an example for others. It is not whether you are modeling but whether you are a good or a bad example for those who are watching. You will be watched and imitated—for better or for worse. Indonesians have a proverb that says, "The coconut doesn't fall far from the tree." In other words, you will reproduce after your own kind. Wise leaders intentionally use their personal example to inspire, motivate, and demonstrate desired behavior or outcomes to others. Never underestimate the power of modeling!

Leaders who follow the same rules as those they supervise, thinking that the rules apply to themselves as well as others, will encourage others to do the same. Leaders who submit to others' authority find that people more willingly submit to their authority. The lifestyle that you choose as a leader will speak loudly about your values, and it will be imitated. Everything about your life and leadership will be scrutinized and conclusions will be drawn—some good and accurate, some not so good and inaccurate. Count on it—don't be surprised when people notice even the smallest details of your life and leadership and imitate them. Seek to intentionally cultivate an example that motivates and inspires others to even greater achievements for Him.

Jesus says, "As you wish that others would do to you, do so to them" (Luke 6:31). We call this the Golden Rule. I have paraphrased this for the Golden Rule of Leadership—"Lead others the way you want to be led." That is, model in your leadership the way you desire others to lead you.

THE POWER OF A CHAMPION

One of the great privileges of leadership is the influence and authority to champion younger, emerging leaders. In my twenties and thirties, I frequently found myself in meetings or being invited as a guest to observe others. Several of my leaders had taken it upon themselves to expose me to these environments. I felt out of my depth at such times, and I certainly wondered, *Why am I here?*

Those exposures were life-changing in so many ways. Just watching other leaders marked me. Yes, I watched them, every aspect of them, taking mental notes. I watched the way they dressed, how they treated others, what type of Bible they used, how they arranged their speaking notes, what they packed for trips, and so on. I peppered them with questions about things big and small, and they patiently answered. That education was invaluable for my development as a leader.

Remember the words of Jesus as He selected the Twelve: "He appointed twelve (whom he also named apostles) so that they might be with him and he might send them out to preach" (Mark 3:14). These emerging leaders were with Jesus as He modeled what He wanted them to become before sending them out to accomplish their mission. Don't neglect to sponsor younger leaders in experiences where exposure to you and others will bless and develop them for future contributions.

THE POWER FOR MAKING EXCEPTIONS

When endeavors are small, no policies or procedures are needed. Issues or questions can be addressed as they arise. But when an enterprise grows, the numbers of questions, problems, and complexities increase, and the need for some standardized procedures and agreed-upon behaviors presents itself. These policies bring efficiencies and allow leaders to focus on innovation and unique problems instead of repeatedly solving the same things.

Policies are helpful, but leadership is an art, not a science. Wise leaders know that there are times when they need to use their leadership power to make an exception to the rules to further the mission or bless someone. Remember, this power for making an exception is for serving others, not for ourselves. Exceptions need to be just that—exceptions, not the new rules. They should be rare and truly needed to address an unusual situation. Don't let your leadership be hamstrung by the policy manual, but don't arbitrarily alter policies without good forethought and counsel. Be transparent when exceptions are made, for hiddenness can be seen as favoritism or as an indication that something is amiss.

A young leader recently came to me asking for financial help to cover the costs of an event he was leading. The amount requested was within my ability to grant, and I was happy to make an exception for him, allocating the money needed to pay for the event. But that gift also came with a reminder that as a steward leader, we must plan our events with a detailed budget that includes not only expenses but also income streams to cover those expenses. We can't have deficit spending on a regular basis. Thus, the exception was made, but the policy was endorsed.

THE POWER OF A SECOND CHANCE

Everyone fails. It was Winston Churchill who said, "Success consists of going from failure to failure without loss of enthusiasm." To expect to succeed every time is to ignore reality. Developmentally, our failures can be more valuable than our successes if they are processed well and learned from. Younger, less experienced leaders may not realize this truth. They may think that mature, experienced leaders are perfect (well, maybe not perfect, but close to it) and that they seldom, if ever, make mistakes. Thus, when they personally experience a leadership failure, they question whether God will ever be able to use them again.

I remember the first time I directed a state-wide conference for The Navigators. I was responsible for printing the invitation and mailing it to the six thousand people on our mailing list. I had been instructed to proof the invitation with another person before printing, but my haste and youthful zeal overcame my caution. When I picked up the finished brochure, to my horror, I realized that I'd forgotten to include the date of the conference on the invitation! Ugh! It does not exactly inspire confidence in your conference team when the leader forgets to put the date on the invitation! Six thousand brochures went into the trash, and I went back to the print shop, this time with a second set of eyes to proof the copy! And now we had no margin in the event budget to cover other unexpected contingencies. I felt like a complete failure.

Next, there came an opportunity to lead housing and registration at a regional-weekend event. I'd been told to expect a turnout of three hundred or so. To my great surprise, several busloads of unregistered people showed up, and I was unprepared to handle this level of un-expected attendance. Staff were asked to sleep in their cars or in the hallways to accommodate the many new attendees. Let's just say that I was not well received as I moved staff out of their rooms to accom-modate the new arrivals!

These instances, and a litany of others, made me question whether I could ever successfully lead an event. But those who were supervis-ing and mentoring me continued to trust me with more responsi-bilities, time and time again, carefully debriefing me afterwards on lessons learned from mistakes that were never to be repeated. Their continued confidence in me began to build a self-confidence that God could indeed use me. Yes, I continued to fail, sometimes embar-rassingly so. Yet my supervisors and champions stuck with me, giving me multiple second chances when I was ready to give up on myself. They believed in me when I found it difficult to believe in myself. I'm so grateful for their trust in God to work in me and for their patience to see that work to maturity.

THE POWER OF PROMOTION

Another type of power that comes with wise leadership is that of promoting others. Wise leaders seek to promote others instead of themselves. Wise leaders will use their authority to position emerging leaders in new opportunities for growth and contribution. They realize that leaders grow when given responsibility, and thus, they promote others into new, challenging roles for their continued development. They believe in the potential of these emerging leaders and hope that they will one day go on to even greater heights than themselves.

These wise leaders recognize that accomplishments are due to the work of many and are quick to acknowledge others' contributions. They generously share the spotlight so that others may get due credit. They never seek to draw attention to themselves, instead humbly admitting that all that they are and have comes as a gift from God. They are not threatened by the giftedness of those around them, for they know that leadership positions are all given by Him. They know that they steward these responsibilities until God chooses to give them to someone else.

The wise leader knows how to exercise power in ways that further God's purposes and promote His glory, not their own. Those they lead thrive—not just survive—under such leadership. Those who exercise their leadership power in leading volunteers find that people continue to voluntarily follow them. As Alexander the Great noted, "I am not afraid of an army of lions led by a sheep; I am afraid of an army of sheep led by a lion."

DEVOTIONAL REFLECTION

BIBLE REFLECTION

Read and reflect on the following passages regarding the wise use of power. Note particularly the applications to life situations.

- Zechariah 4:6

- Galatians 2:20

- Luke 4:1, 14

PRAYER ITEMS

- Ask God to remind you to regularly practice affirmation. Ask Him to help you genuinely affirm, not flatter, others.

- Begin regularly asking God to anoint you and fill you with His Spirit to help you lead with wisdom and in His power.

PERSONAL APPLICATIONS

- Read and meditate on the three temptations of Jesus in Luke 4:1-15. Reflect on your own life and leadership and how the enemy works to tempt you in these areas. Are there changes that God is asking you to make?

- When was the last time you had a real vacation? Do you have a sense that you can't be gone or things will fall apart while you are away? Plan some time off and delegate authority and responsibility to others while you are gone. Truly take a break; don't check in to see how things are going when you are away.

Conclusion

THE CHARACTERISTICS
OF GODLY WISDOM

The wisdom that comes from heaven is first of all pure; then peace-loving,
considerate, submissive, full of mercy and good fruit, impartial and sincere.
JAMES 3:17, NIV

Wisdom is justified by her deeds.
MATTHEW 11:19

HOW DOES SOMEONE know if they have wisdom? What does godly wisdom look like in leadership? As stated previously, wisdom can frequently be seen in retrospect: "Wisdom is proved right by all her children" (Luke 7:35, NIV). But is it possible to recognize wisdom in the present moment? Is there any way to evaluate one's own progress in this pursuit or to see it in the lives of those we mentor? And should we begin pursuing wisdom as we are encouraged to do in Proverbs, how do we know if we are on the pathway to obtaining it?

The book of James exhorts us to ask God for wisdom if we sense we are lacking it (James 1:5), but it also gives us insight into wisdom's characteristics in our lives. These manifestations of wisdom can be used as a self-evaluation and as a means for intentionally helping others to grow in their wisdom. Seven characteristics of wisdom are found in James 3:17: Godly wisdom is *pure, peace-loving, considerate, submissive, full of mercy and good fruit, impartial,* and *sincere.*

Let's look at these characteristics and see how we can use them to evaluate progress in pursuing wisdom.

PURE

The first characteristic of godly wisdom is that it is *pure.* By pure we mean clean, uncontaminated, undefiled, not polluted, and holy. The world has its own wisdom based on experience. When assessing the world's wisdom, we must compare it with God's wisdom. Wisdom from above discerns the ways of the world from the ways of God and, where they are in conflict, rejects the world's beliefs and values. It does not conform to the patterns of this world but is renewed by the truth of God's Word. Godly wisdom uses the Word of God as the unchanging standard and rule for life and leadership and willingly submits to its authority.

James reminds us that "religion that is pure and undefiled before God the Father is this: to visit orphans and widows in their affliction, and to keep oneself unstained from the world" (James 1:27). Note how the purity of godly wisdom works itself out into practical behavior that honors God and aligns with His character.

PEACE-LOVING

The second characteristic of God's wisdom is that it is *peace-loving.* Wise leaders build harmony—not divisions, factions, or a party spirit—as they lead. Godly wisdom is not pugilistic in nature. It is not afraid of conflict and will not shrink back from any attack on God's ways or righteousness. It uses power for good and will always stand for what is right.

Paul addresses this in Corinth, where he chastises the believers for their party spirit. He says,

I, brothers, could not address you as spiritual people, but as people of the flesh, as infants in Christ. I fed you with milk, not solid food, for you were not ready for it. And even now you are not yet ready, for you are still of the flesh. For while there is jealousy and strife among you, are you not of the flesh and behaving only in a human way? For when one says, "I follow Paul," and another, "I follow Apollos," are you not being merely human?

I CORINTHIANS 3:1-4

This characteristic of wisdom seeks unity in the Spirit and to live at peace with everyone, if possible (Romans 12:18).

CONSIDERATE

Third, godly wisdom is *considerate*. It is kind and gentle with others. It is not harsh or mean-spirited. It is sensitive to its own weaknesses, especially when seeing those weaknesses in others. It is not judgmental, and it seeks the best for others. Wisdom seeks to place others before self in all areas of life and service. It is not self-promoting. Paul reminds the Philippians to "Do nothing from selfish ambition or conceit, but in humility count others more significant than yourselves. Let each of you look not only to his own interests, but also to the interests of others" (Philippians 2:3-4).

Jesus speaks to this kind of practical wisdom in the Sermon on the Mount:

Judge not, that you be not judged. For with the judgment you pronounce you will be judged, and with the measure you use it will be measured to you. Why do you see the speck that is in your brother's eye, but do not notice the log that is in your own eye? Or how can you say to your brother, "Let me take the speck out of your eye," when there is the log in your own eye? You hypocrite, first take the log out of your own eye, and then you will see clearly to take the speck out of your brother's eye.

MATTHEW 7:1-5

And Paul reminds Timothy how to address opposition:

The Lord's servant must not be quarrelsome but kind to everyone, able to teach, patiently enduring evil, correcting his opponents with gentleness. God may perhaps grant them repentance leading to a knowledge of the truth, and they may come to their senses and escape from the snare of the devil, after being captured by him to do his will.

2 TIMOTHY 2:24-26

SUBMISSIVE

Fourth, godly wisdom from above is *submissive*. This wisdom submits itself first to God as Lord in all areas of life and leadership. It submits itself to the authority of God's Word. Trusting in God's sovereignty, it submits to the authority of earthly governments, recognizing that these worldly leaders are established by Him. And this godly wisdom means that we submit to spiritual leaders, for they are appointed by God to watch over us and care for us (Hebrews 13:17).

Jesus spoke to this when queried whether it was right to pay taxes to Caesar. He said, "Render to Caesar the things that are Caesar's, and to God the things that are God's" (Mark 12:17). Paul, speaking about similar themes, says, "Let every person be subject to the governing authorities. For there is no authority except from God, and those that exist have been instituted by God" (Romans 13:1). And Peter says, "Honor everyone. Love the brotherhood. Fear God. Honor the emperor" (1 Peter 2:17).

FULL OF MERCY AND GOOD FRUIT

The fifth characteristic of God's wisdom is that it's *full of mercy and good fruit*. This wisdom has compassion on the downcast, the hurting, and the marginalized and seeks to help them in their distress. This wisdom loves and accepts others unconditionally, just as God loves us. It does what is right, not what is culturally expected or expedient. It lives a life that is blameless and does not give others opportunity for slandering the King or His Kingdom.

Jesus again addressed this when He was questioned about His association with tax collectors and sinners—those who were deemed "unclean" by society. He wisely responded, "It is not the healthy who need a doctor, but the sick. But go and learn what this means: 'I desire mercy, not sacrifice.' For I have not come to call the righteous, but sinners" (Matthew 9:12-13, NIV). Peter, speaking of Jesus' lifestyle, describes "how God anointed Jesus of Nazareth with the Holy Spirit and power, and how he went around doing good and healing all who were under the power of the devil, because God was with him" (Acts 10:38, NIV). And Paul reminds those who follow Jesus, "Let us not become weary in doing good, for at the proper time we will reap a harvest if we do not give up. Therefore, as we have opportunity, let us do good to all people, especially to those who belong to the family of believers" (Galatians 6:9-10, NIV).

IMPARTIAL

Sixth, we see that God's wisdom is *impartial*. Those with godly wisdom do not show favoritism to anyone, regardless of ethnicity, age, gender, or socioeconomic class. In particular, they avoid showing favoritism to family members and friends. Wisdom manifests itself in one who is fair and just. This impartiality is consistently demonstrated in all contexts of life and leadership.

We return to James for more practical instructions on this characteristic of wisdom. He exhorts us:

> My brothers, show no partiality as you hold the faith in our
> Lord Jesus Christ, the Lord of glory. For if a man wearing a
> gold ring and fine clothing comes into your assembly, and a
> poor man in shabby clothing also comes in, and if you pay
> attention to the one who wears the fine clothing and say,
> "You sit here in a good place," while you say to the poor man,
> "You stand over there," or, "Sit down at my feet," have you
> not then made distinctions among yourselves and become
> judges with evil thoughts? Listen, my beloved brothers, has
> not God chosen those who are poor in the world to be rich
> in faith and heirs of the kingdom, which he has promised to
> those who love him? But you have dishonored the poor man.
> Are not the rich the ones who oppress you, and the ones who
> drag you into court? Are they not the ones who blaspheme the
> honorable name by which you were called?
>
> If you really fulfill the royal law according to the
> Scripture, "You shall love your neighbor as yourself," you are
> doing well. But if you show partiality, you are committing
> sin and are convicted by the law as transgressors.
>
> JAMES 2:1-9

SINCERE

The seventh and final characteristic of God's wisdom is that it is *sincere*. This kind of wisdom is not duplicitous in word or deed. Consistent integrity of words and deeds are demonstrated in every situation. This person walks the talk. Authenticity is the quality of this life.

Jesus' enemies used His integrity to try trapping Him. "They came and said to him, 'Teacher, we know that you are true and do not care about anyone's opinion. For you are not swayed by appearances, but truly teach the way of God. Is it lawful to pay taxes to Caesar, or not?" (Mark 12:14). What an amazing testimony concerning Jesus' integrity. He was so known as a man of integrity that even His enemies tried to use this quality against Him! By contrast, the hypocrisy of the religious leaders drew Jesus' ire, as in His teaching to the crowds in Matthew 23:2-3: "The scribes and the Pharisees sit on Moses' seat, so do and observe whatever they tell you, but not the works they do. For they preach, but do not practice."

By reflecting on these seven characteristics of godly wisdom in the life of an individual, we can know if we are making progress in our pursuit. While we may never totally arrive, we can note progress in our life and in the life of someone we are mentoring. These qualities are mile markers enabling us to see increments of change as we seek to grow in wisdom and help others do the same.

DEVOTIONAL REFLECTION

BIBLE REFLECTION

Read and reflect on the following passages regarding the various characteristics of wisdom. Note particularly the applications to life situations.

- Colossians 2:2-3

- Colossians 2:20-23

- Hebrews 12:1-2

PRAYER ITEMS

- Ask God to help you separate yourself from sin patterns or from other hindrances in your life that are preventing you from running your race well.

- Ask God to help you humbly submit to the authorities He has placed over you.

PERSONAL APPLICATIONS

- What random act of kindness can you do that no one other than you and God will know about? Do it this week.

- Consider asking someone to mentor you for development in an area of life or leadership.

EPILOGUE

WHEN WE FIRST went to Indonesia, we spent almost two years in formal language study, seeking to become communicative (certainly far from fluent) in a foreign language. My wife, Dana, and I went to the language school each morning to learn new vocabulary and memorize a few new sayings. My first day's memorized dialog was "Hi. My name is Tom. I'm studying the Indonesian language." Then, after lunch, we walked the streets around our house, repeating these phrases to as many people as possible. This language-learning process consisted of gaining a little new material every day and then using it a lot over a long period of time. We not only worked on what to say in our new language but also how to say it. Over time, we grew more and more comfortable expressing ourselves in this second language.

Our pursuit of wisdom is like this language-learning process. We begin with familiarizing ourselves with what wisdom consists of—the definition of terms; becoming familiar with new vocabulary. Then, as we build vocabulary, we also practice what we are learning in real-life leadership situations. Throughout this book, we have addressed various components of wisdom and built vocabulary to begin communicating about it. But this is just a beginning.

Becoming a wise leader is a noble, lifelong pursuit. Today's complexity of leadership and rapid pace of change demand wisdom from above. The more responsibility a leader has, the greater the complexity of their leadership demands and the corresponding increased need for more wisdom. The rapid pace of life calls for agility and the ability to think on your feet. One small error is quickly magnified. Wisdom for leaders is at a premium today more than ever.

Growing in godly wisdom results in aligning with God's purposes in and through us. As Kingdom leaders, those of us who pursue His wisdom will find His Spirit guiding us as we lead. Following His wisdom is not a guarantee for success from the world's perspective, but it will result in the Lord's pronouncement of "Well done, good and faithful servant" (Matthew 25:23).

Godly wisdom moves toward practical application in life and leadership. As our beliefs become rooted in His ways and His truth, our values align with His Kingdom values. These values then guide choices that result in behavior that honors Him. May the ripple impact of our lives be such that wisdom is manifested through our influence, whether personal or organizational. And may any good that comes be to His credit and not our own.

ACKNOWLEDGMENTS

I WOULD LIKE TO EXPRESS my deep appreciation for all those who modeled, inspired, and taught me what it means to be a wise leader.

In particular, I would like to thank my wife, Dana, as well as Lee Maschhoff, Jerry Bridges, Dr. Bobby Clinton, Jelle Jongsma, Dr. Erwin Lutzer, Dr. Doug Nuenke, Bpk. Badu Situmorang, Doug Sparks, Paul Stanley, Mike Treneer, and Dr. Jerry White for pointing the way to wisdom by their lives and leadership.

Appendix

WISDOM-DEVELOPMENT
RESOURCES

BIBLE STUDY

The following topical Bible studies are designed to help you grow in your understanding and convictions related to the various aspects of godly wisdom.

The Foundation of Wisdom

Read the following passages and make any observations you can regarding the development of wisdom in our lives. Note particularly the contrast between worldly wisdom and God's wisdom and the applications of wisdom to life situations.

- Exodus 33:12-14
- Job 28:20-24
- Psalm 111:10
- Psalm 119:99-100
- Proverbs 1:7
- Proverbs 8:10-11
- Proverbs 9:10

In the following passages, note any observations about the godly wisdom given to Daniel and how he pursued wisdom as contrasted with the worldly wisdom of the king's advisors.

- Daniel 1:17-20
- Daniel 2:24-30
- Daniel 5:10-17
- Daniel 9:1-3, 20-23

Review the following passages regarding Jesus' teaching about wisdom and its pursuit. Note the comparisons of worldly wisdom with godly wisdom.

- Matthew 7:24-27
- Matthew 10:16
- Matthew 16:5-12
- Matthew 17:10-13

In the following passages, Paul contrasts worldly and godly wisdom. Note any similarities and differences between the two.

- 1 Corinthians 1:22-31
- 1 Corinthians 2:6-16

What do the following passages teach us about the source and pursuit of godly wisdom?

- Ephesians 1:17
- James 1:5

Prudence

Read the following passages and make any observations you can regarding prudence. Note particularly the applications of prudence to life situations.

- Proverbs 12:16
- Proverbs 12:23
- Proverbs 14:8
- Proverbs 14:15

- Proverbs 15:5
- Proverbs 19:14
- Proverbs 22:3

PRUDENCE DEMONSTRATED

Review the following passages and note how prudence is illustrated in the actions and lives mentioned in the passage.

- 1 Samuel 25:1-35
- 2 Kings 5:1-19
- Proverbs 23:1-3
- Proverbs 24:27
- Ecclesiastes 9:4
- Matthew 7:6
- Matthew 22:15-22
- Matthew 25:1-13
- Matthew 25:14-30
- Luke 14:28-32
- Luke 20:1-8
- Acts 23:1-10

Read Proverbs 6:6-11. What can be learned from the ant, who stores provision ahead of time, and how does this relate to prudence?

Knowledge

Read the following passages and make any observations you can regarding godly knowledge. Note particularly the applications of knowledge to life situations.

GODLY KNOWLEDGE

- Proverbs 10:14
- Ecclesiastes 2:26
- 1 Corinthians 12:4-11
- 1 Timothy 6:20-21

KNOWING GOD

Our God is an awesome God. What can you observe in the following passages regarding knowing God?

- Psalm 46:10
- John 1:18
- John 10:25-38
- John 17:3
- Ephesians 1:17
- Colossians 1:15

KNOWING GOD'S WAYS

The ways of God are the motive and reasoning behind the acts of God. They explain the *Why?* of God's actions. What do you see in the following passages regarding God's ways?

- Exodus 33:12-13
- Psalm 25:4
- Psalm 95:6-11
- Psalm 103:7
- Isaiah 55:8-9

KNOWING GOD'S WORD

We want to know God's Word because it is the revelation of God Himself to us, His creation. Review the following passages and note what is said about God's Word.

- Psalm 119:97-99
- Isaiah 55:10-11
- Matthew 22:29
- John 17:6-8
- 2 Timothy 2:15
- 2 Timothy 3:16-17
- Hebrews 4:12

MEDITATING ON GOD'S WORD

To meditate on God's Word is to think deeply about and seek how it might apply to our life. What do the following passages say about meditating on God's Word?

- Joshua 1:8
- Psalm 1:1-3
- Psalm 119:15-16
- Psalm 119:148

KNOWLEDGE DEMONSTRATED

Read 1 Corinthians 2:6-16 and note any observations related to the knowledge of God and how to obtain it.

Discretion

Read the following passages and make any observations regarding the use of discretion. Note particularly the applications of discretion in life situations.

- Proverbs 1:4
- Proverbs 2:11
- Proverbs 11:22
- Acts 16:1-4
- Acts 17:22-23
- Acts 23:6-8
- 2 Corinthians 12:1-6
- 1 Timothy 2:9, 15

Jesus taught and modeled discretion. What do that following passages say about the wise use of discretion?

- Matthew 7:6
- Matthew 17:24-27
- Luke 20:20-25
- Matthew 15:10-15

- Matthew 17:27-28
- Matthew 23:1-7

DISCRETION DEMONSTRATED

Read 2 Corinthians 8:16-21 and make any observations related to Paul's use of discretion and how it was demonstrated in the collection and distribution of money for the poor in Jerusalem.

Counsel

Read the following passages and make any observations you can regarding counsel—both giving and receiving it. Note particularly the results of responding to wise and unwise counsel.

- Genesis 3:1-19
- Matthew 7:24-27
- 2 Samuel 15:32-36; 17:5-16
- 1 Kings 12:1-17
- Ezra 10:1-12
- Job 29:21-25
- Psalm 1:1-3
- Psalm 73:23-24
- Proverbs 1:22-33
- Proverbs 3:5-6
- Proverbs 12:15
- Proverbs 15:22
- Proverbs 19:20
- Ecclesiastes 4:13

ACCEPTING AND REJECTING WISE COUNSEL
- Genesis 41:25-40
- Daniel 4:24-37

ACCEPTING AND REJECTING UNWISE COUNSEL
Review Luke 12:13-21 (the parable of the rich fool) and make any

WISDOM-DEVELOPMENT RESOURCES

observations related to the man in the parable: the counsel he takes, the source of his counsel, and how acting on that counsel brought certain outcomes in his life.

Sound Judgment

Read Genesis 41:14-16, 33, 37-40 about the life and leadership of Joseph. What observations can you make about how Joseph exercised sound judgment?

Read the following passages and make any observations you can regarding the wisdom quality of sound judgment—both in your life and in your leadership.

- Leviticus 10:8-11
- 1 Samuel 16:7
- 1 Kings 3:7-13
- 1 Chronicles 12:23, 32
- Psalm 119:105
- Ecclesiastes 7:19
- Ecclesiastes 9:17-18
- Isaiah 30:21

What do the following verses from Proverbs say about the importance of wisdom and its application in sound judgment?

- Proverbs 1:1-33
- Proverbs 2:6-8
- Proverbs 18:1
- Proverbs 19:20
- Proverbs 28:11

What do the following passages say about the place of wisdom and sound judgment in the life of a disciple of Christ?

- 2 Corinthians 12:9
- Philippians 1:9-10
- 1 John 4:1-3

Understanding

Read the following verses and note Moses' requests for understanding from the Lord. What was granted to him as a result?

- Exodus 33:12-14
- Psalm 103:7

In the following passages, note how Jesus addressed the disciples' lack of understanding. How did He help them grow in understanding, what did they grow to understand, and how does this apply to His followers today?

- Matthew 16:5-12
- Matthew 17:10-13
- Mark 4:1-20
- Mark 4:30-34
- Luke 24:45

Read the following passages and make any observations you can regarding the wisdom quality of understanding—both in your life and in leadership.

- Job 12:12-13
- Psalm 119:97-100
- Proverbs 2:6
- Proverbs 3:5-6
- Proverbs 4:5-7
- Isaiah 55:8-9
- 1 Corinthians 3:19-23
- Colossians 1:9-10
- Hebrews 12:1-2

- James 3:13
- 1 John 5:20

Power

Read the following passages and make any observations you can regarding the wise use of power—both in your life and leadership.

- Zechariah 4:6
- Psalm 62:11-12
- Matthew 28:19-20
- Luke 4:1, 14
- Galatians 2:20
- Philippians 4:13
- 1 Corinthians 4:1-7
- 1 Corinthians 4:14-21
- Ephesians 4:29, 32
- Ephesians 5:15-20
- Ephesians 6:10

TEMPTATIONS OF JESUS

Review the three temptations of Jesus in Luke 4:1-15. Note how the devil sought to tempt Jesus in the abuse of His power and how unwise leaders are tempted in the same way today.

REHOBOAM VS. JEROBOAM

Read 1 Kings 12:1-19 regarding the leadership of Rehoboam. Note how he used his positional leadership authority and power. How are unwise leaders tempted to do similar things today?

Characteristics of Godly Wisdom

Read the following passages and make any observations you can regarding the manifestations of godly wisdom in one's life and leadership.

GODLY WISDOM
- Colossians 2:2-3
- Colossians 2:20-23
- Colossians 4:5-6

PURE
- 2 Corinthians 7:1
- Hebrews 12:1-2
- James 1:27

PEACE-LOVING
- Romans 12:18
- 1 Corinthians 3:1-4

CONSIDERATE
- Matthew 7:1-5
- Philippians 4:5

SUBMISSIVE
- Ephesians 5:21
- Hebrews 13:17

FULL OF MERCY AND GOOD FRUIT
- Matthew 9:13
- 1 John 3:16-18

IMPARTIAL
- Exodus 23:2-3
- James 2:1, 9

SINCERE
- 1 Chronicles 29:17
- Mark 12:13-14

MEMORY VERSES

The following suggested memory verses are arranged by chapter topics for storing the Word of God in your heart. The Holy Spirit will then remind you of these passages as you encounter daily situations where you need wisdom from above.

The Foundation of Godly Wisdom

- Psalm 119:99-100
- Proverbs 1:7
- Proverbs 8:11
- James 1:5

Prudence

- Proverbs 12:23
- Proverbs 14:8
- Proverbs 14:15
- Proverbs 15:5

Knowledge

- John 17:3
- Psalm 103:7
- Isaiah 55:10-11
- 2 Timothy 3:16-17

Discretion

- Proverbs 2:11
- Proverbs 11:22
- Matthew 7:6
- John 11:42

Counsel

- Proverbs 15:22
- Proverbs 19:20

- Ecclesiastes 4:13
- Matthew 7:24

Sound Judgment

- 1 Samuel 16:7
- Isaiah 30:21
- Psalm 119:105
- 2 Corinthians 12:9

Understanding

- Proverbs 3:5-6
- Proverbs 4:5-7
- Isaiah 55:8-9
- James 3:13

Power

- Zechariah 4:6
- Ephesians 6:10
- Philippians 4:13
- 1 Corinthians 4:20

Characteristics of Godly Wisdom

- Mark 12:13-14
- 2 Corinthians 7:1
- James 1:27
- James 4:17

Here are some helpful suggestions to aid your memorization process, taken from the NavPress resource *Beginning the Walk*:

1. Write the verse on a 3 × 5 card. Include the reference.
2. Read it frequently.

3. Memorize it one phrase at a time until you can remember the whole statement.

4. Practice saying the verse from memory. Quote the reference at the beginning and end.

5. Review the verse every day for seven weeks.

6. Share the verse—and what it means to you—with a friend or mentor.[1]

PRAYER SUGGESTIONS

The following are some practical suggestions for prayer as you begin pursuing godly wisdom. While there are several in this list, choose a few to begin with, and pray regularly about them.

The Foundation of Godly Wisdom

- Ask God to reveal to you a growing self-awareness regarding the need for His wisdom in your life and leadership.

- Ask Him for discernment to see where you may have mixed worldly wisdom with His wisdom. What does He want you to do about it?

- Are you spending enough time in God's Word for your own growth and development as a wise leader? Ask God to give you an increased hunger for His Word.

- Ask God to show you Kingdom principles as they appear in stories of leadership in the Scriptures.

- Ask God for understanding regarding His ways, just as Moses did in Exodus 33:12-14. Ask for a deeper understanding of His character and how He manifests this character in His actions.

- Are you intentionally developing yourself into a wise leader? Ask the Lord to show you how to be more intentional in your pursuit of godly knowledge, understanding, and wisdom.

- Pray over your recent leadership decisions. Does the Lord bring to mind any situation where you were unwise from God's perspective? What is He asking you to do about it?

The Companions of Godly Wisdom

PRUDENCE

In addition to asking God to make you a person who demonstrates prudence, here are some ideas to help stimulate your prayers in this area. Pray regularly about them.

- Ask God to reveal to you a growing self-awareness regarding prudence in your life and leadership.

- Pray over your recent leadership decisions. Does the Lord brings to mind any situation where there was a lack of prudence on your part? What is He asking you to do about it?

- Are you preparing for your next season of life now? Are you thinking far enough ahead and making decisions today that are preparing you for continuing contribution in the future? Ask God what development goals He has for you to prepare you for this future.

- Are you beginning to mentor someone as your potential replacement? Pray for discernment regarding who the Lord would have you begin investing in for the future.

- Ask God to search your heart for any instances where you have not been prudent with your words. Perhaps you spoke too quickly or did not think carefully about the consequences of your words' impact on others. Is there something that you need to do to make it right?

- Ask God to show you what you have been procrastinating about and what you should begin to act on this week. What actions does He want you to take today on these things?

- Ask the Lord to create within you a teachable spirit that will enable you to learn from everyone, not just from a few selected sources.

- Ask the Lord to help you become more aware of when you are talking too much or when you should be asking questions instead of sharing your thoughts.

- Ask God to show you how you can better invest His resources of people and money for greater return for His glory.

KNOWLEDGE

In addition to asking God to make you a person who is filled with godly knowledge, here are some ideas to help stimulate your prayers in pursuing knowledge. Pray regularly over them.

- Ask God to reveal to you a growing self-awareness regarding the importance and application of knowledge in your life and leadership.

- Are you beginning to mentor someone? Have you approached them with questions and a desire to know them, or have you come with answers and a desire to teach them? Pray about your attitude as you mentor them.

- Ask God to give you a hunger for knowing Him that will overcome a lack of self-discipline or laziness as you engage in His Word.

- Are you facing any decisions that you need more detailed knowledge about before you can decide? Ask God to give you all the knowledge you need and then guide you in making a wise decision.

- Pray over some of your Scripture-memory verses and meditate on them, asking God to help you personally apply them.

- Ask God to reveal Himself to you in a new, fresh, and deeper way than before.

DISCRETION

In addition to asking God to make you a person who demonstrates discretion, here are some ideas to help stimulate your prayers in this area. Pray regularly about them.

- Ask God to reveal to you a growing self-awareness regarding the importance and application of discretion in your life and leadership.

- Pray over your recent leadership team discussions. Does the Lord bring to mind any situation where there was a lack of discretion on your part? Did you dominate the discussion or cut it short by sharing your opinions? What is He asking you to do about it?

- Ask God to teach you discretion before you speak and help you grow in awareness of how you affect those around you after you speak.

- Are you beginning to mentor someone? Have you approached them with questions and a desire to know them or come with answers and a desire to teach them? Pray about your attitude as you mentor them.

- Does the Lord bring to mind someone whom you have offended by your lack of discretion? What does He want you to do about it?

- Pray over the next two weeks of your schedule. Ask the Lord to show you where you can proactively prepare for and demonstrate discretion in these coming events.

- Are you working in a cross-cultural or multigenerational situation? Ask God to show you how to be more discreet in this environment.

- Do you routinely share too much when talking with others? Ask God for self-awareness of when you have shared enough and self-control not to go beyond that limit.

- The next time you find yourself in a group discussion, ask the Lord to help you be aware of what He wants you to share, when He wants you to speak, and how He wants you to share.

The Competencies of Godly Wisdom

COUNSEL

In addition to asking God to make you a person who gives and receives wise counsel, here are some ideas to help stimulate your prayers for growing in this area. Pray regularly about them.

- Ask God to reveal to you a growing self-awareness regarding the importance and application of wise counsel in your life and leadership.

- Ask God to teach you how to give wise counsel, especially counsel from the Bible.

- Pray and reflect over your past two weeks of interactions with acquaintances and family. Are there any areas where you have not listened to counsel that you now think you should reconsider? Or did you accept counsel that you now consider dubious? What does God want you to do about it?

• Are you beginning to mentor someone? Have you approached this relationship with answers and a desire to tell them what to be or do? Pray about your attitude as you mentor them.

• Does the Lord bring to mind someone whom you should go to and ask for counsel regarding an area of your life or leadership? What does He want you to do?

• Pray over the next two weeks of your schedule. Ask the Lord to show you where you can proactively prepare for and demonstrate either giving or receiving counsel in these coming events.

• The next time you are in a team meeting and discussion, prayerfully reflect, asking the Lord to show you when to speak your opinions and how to share them.

• Husbands, the next time you must make an important decision, ask to pray with your wife about it and listen carefully to her counsel.

• Ask God to counsel you from His Word as you seek to make any life decision. Ask for His guidance as you face decisions with multiple options or differing opinions.

SOUND JUDGMENT

In addition to asking God to make you a person who consistently exercises sound judgment, here are some ideas to stimulate your prayers for growing in this area. Pray regularly about them.

• Ask God to reveal to you a growing self-awareness regarding the importance and application of sound judgment in your life and leadership.

- Pray over your recent leadership-team discussions. Does the Lord bring to mind any situation where you did not exercise sound judgment? Did you rush to decide without adequate information or without thinking through long-term consequences? What is He asking you to do about it?

- Ask God to teach you how to exercise sound judgment in problem-solving.

- After arriving at a solution to a current problem, stop and ask the Lord to show you two or more additional solutions to the same problem. Ask Him to then show you which one of these possible solutions is His best.

- Are you currently supervising someone? Are you solving problems for them that they should be learning to solve for themselves? Pray about how best to help those you supervise grow in sound judgment.

- Is there a decision you need to make that you've procrastinated about because you don't know what to do? Pray about whom you should ask for counsel regarding this issue.

- Make a list of the problems that need to be addressed and decisions that you must make in the next few months. Ask the Lord to show you insights into leverage points, direction, or possible consequences as you seek solutions to these challenges.

- Ask the Lord to give you faith and courage to face the pressure of conforming to the world and the cultural tide of the day.

- Ask the Lord for the ability to make the complex simple. Ask Him also for the ability to communicate this simplicity to others in ways that help them see it as clearly as you do.

UNDERSTANDING

In addition to asking God to make you a person who exercises wise understanding, here are some ideas to help stimulate your prayers for growing in this area. Pray regularly about them.

- Ask God to reveal to you a growing self-awareness regarding the importance and application of wise understanding in your life and leadership.

- Ask God to teach you His ways, just as He did with Moses (see Exodus 33:12-17).

- Pray and reflect over your recent leadership-team discussions. Does the Lord bring to mind any situation where you did not exercise understanding by stopping long enough to reflect on the situation fully? Did you rush to a decision without adequate information or without thinking through long-term consequences? What is He asking you to do about it?

- Ask God to teach you how to correlate individual facts and data points. Ask Him to show you trends and cultural changes as they happen and in retrospect.

- Are you supervising someone? Are you helping them grow in understanding of themselves and their context? Do you know their God-given design temperament? Pray about how best to help them grow in understanding through your supervision.

- Is there a decision that you've procrastinated in making because you don't sense that you have enough information? Pray, asking the Lord what more is needed for you to make that decision. What does He want you to do to get this information?

- What recurring or long-standing problem have you not been able to solve? Ask God for understanding in how to bring a lasting solution.

- Ask God to help you grow in emotional intelligence, becoming more aware of your own emotional state and the emotional state of those around you. Ask Him to help you understand how to better express those emotions to others.

- Ask God to help you grow in the spiritual discipline of meditating on His Word. Ask Him for insights and understanding as you reflect on the Scriptures.

POWER

In addition to asking God to make you a person who exercises power wisely, here are some ideas to help stimulate your prayers for growing in this area. Pray regularly about them.

- Ask God to reveal to you a growing self-awareness regarding the importance and application of wisely using power in your life and leadership.

- Pray and reflect over your recent leadership-team discussions. Does the Lord bring to mind any situation where you did not exercise power well? Did you dominate the discussion or demand your way in a decision? What is He asking you to do about it?

- Ask God to remind you to regularly practice affirmation. Ask Him to help you to genuinely affirm—not flatter—others.

- Are you supervising someone? Are you empowering them with authority to do their job or are you keeping that power for yourself? Pray about how best to help them grow in the wise use of authority through your supervision.

- Ask God to show you where you tend to rely on your own authority and power instead of on His. What does He want you to do differently?

- Ask the Lord to show you someone He wants you to champion (or perhaps, for you to give a second chance). What does He want you to do about this?

- Begin to regularly ask God to anoint you and fill you with His Spirit to help you lead with wisdom and in His power.

- Pray and reflect over the idea of transitioning your leadership position to someone else. What steps can you take now to begin that process? What does He want you to do about it?

- Ask God to show you where you may have taken credit for something that was due to someone else's contribution. What does He want you to do about it?

Characteristics of Godly Wisdom

Ask God to make you a person who grows in wisdom and manifests these seven characteristics. Pray regularly about these seven qualities, asking Him to help you grow in self-awareness of where and how they can be demonstrated in your life and leadership.

EXERCISES FOR DEVELOPING GODLY WISDOM

Here are some practical exercises to help you grow in pursuing wisdom. Select one or two to begin with and put into practice what the Lord has been speaking to you about regarding your growth in godly wisdom. These suggested exercises are general and may not address your specific needs or concerns. How specifically could you practice pursuing godly wisdom over the next week?

The Foundation of Wisdom

- Ask for feedback in this area from those you lead. Let them know that you want to grow in the quality of wisdom and need their help. Define for them the difference between knowledge, understanding, and wisdom, with specific manifestations of how they might be demonstrated in leadership. Ask them for their thoughts and ideas. Just knowing that their leader is seeking to grow in this area will be inspirational and motivational to all who follow your leadership!

- What are you currently reading? What's in your to-read pile? Do these books demonstrate a pursuit of God's wisdom or the world's? Consider reading a biography of a great Christian leader whom God used to deeply impact their generation.

- At your next leadership-team meeting, ask the team to list Bible passages that have a bearing on a pressing problem. Lead the team in prayer for wisdom as you seek to solve the problem.

- As in all things, our adversary in the pursuit of Kingdom wisdom is the devil—the father of lies and master of deceit. A key protection against deception is awareness. Pray with your team, asking God to show you where you are all being lied to or possibly deceived by the evil one.

- Is there someone you know that you consider wise in an area of life or leadership? Ask them to mentor you in this area for a period of time. When you meet with them, ask them specific questions that can help you learn the wisdom they have gained.

- Is the pursuit of wisdom truly precious in your sight? What schedule changes do you need to make to demonstrate that this value is real and not just a good idea?

- Are you intentionally passing the wisdom God has given you to others? Are you building into your children the high value of pursuing wisdom? Are you intentionally passing to your children or grandchildren the practical wisdom of life and leadership that He has given you? What does He want you to do about it? Whom could you meet with in the next week to begin investing in, passing your wisdom to others?

- Are you developing a leadership bench—a pool of emerging leaders to take significant roles in the future? Are you preparing them to become wise leaders? Do you know a younger or less experienced leader under your influence whom you could begin intentionally helping grow in their leadership understanding and skill? Make an appointment with them and share some leadership principles that you think would benefit them.

- Read the Gospels regularly, looking for how Jesus built knowledge, understanding, and wisdom into the lives of His disciples. How can you imitate His example?

The Companions of Godly Wisdom

PRUDENCE

Here are some practical exercises to help you grow in the area of prudence.

- Ask for feedback in this area from those you lead. Let them know that you want to grow in the quality of prudence and need their help. Define for them specific manifestations of how prudence might be demonstrated in leadership and ask them for their thoughts. Consider making the feedback anonymous or to a third party so that people are free to be honest. Just knowing that their leader is seeking to grow in this area will be inspirational and motivational to all who follow your leadership!

- Read and meditate on the book of Proverbs, asking God to show you specific applications of how to integrate prudence into your daily life and leadership.

- Risk assessment is a key aspect of leadership. What decision or issue are you currently facing? Evaluate the potential risk associated with this issue—both short-term and long-term risks to your mission. What are the potential benefits from this decision?

- Discernment is a related aspect of leadership. What long-term issue is once again coming to the forefront of your attention? Discuss it with key associates and seek to discern root causes that can be addressed to produce a lasting solution.

- What current trend or future change do you see now that will significantly affect you and your mission? What would be prudent to do now to prepare for this change?

- Are you managing your personal and missional finances prudently? Should you ask a financial advisor to review your current financial situation and offer advice?

- Are you developing yourself as a leader? Do you have a personal-development plan with developmental goals? What can you begin doing today to intentionally develop yourself as a leader?

- Do you have a succession plan for future leadership? What can you begin doing today to prepare for future leadership transitions?

- Read the Gospels and Acts. Look for examples where Jesus, Paul, and other leaders demonstrated prudence in their daily lives to help you grow in self-awareness.

KNOWLEDGE

Here are some practical exercises to help you grow in the area of pursuing godly knowledge.

- Create or review your own Core Set of Bible books, passages, characters, or topics where you will begin concentrating your study, memory work, reading, and devotions. If you have a Core Set already, are changes needed—either adding to or deleting from the set?

- Begin doing your daily devotions and your personal Bible study in your Core Set.

- Discernment is also a key aspect of leadership and is frequently linked with knowledge. What long-term, unresolved issue is coming to the forefront of your attention? What can you learn from the past related to this issue? What biblical principles and truth apply to this situation? Discuss this issue with key associates and seek to discern root causes that can be addressed to produce lasting change.

- As a leader, what can you do to create a learning environment that promotes knowing God, His ways, and His Word? Are you personally modeling a pursuit of knowing God? Are you creating opportunities for others to know Him and His Word more deeply?

- Implement a Bible-reading program that will take you through the entire Bible or the entire New Testament. Or consider reading through an entire book of the Bible multiple times in the next month.

- Are you keeping a written record of what God is teaching you about Himself and His ways? Consider keeping a personal journal to record your daily-devotional thoughts or life lessons that He reveals to you. Show God that you are paying attention!

- Take an objective look at those around you from whom you take counsel. Are some of them "contrarian voices," or have you surrounded yourself with people who almost always agree with you? Ask your team if they feel free to disagree with you. Ask them what you can do to promote more open, frank discussions of all viewpoints among team members.

DISCRETION

Here are some practical exercises to help you grow in the area of discretion.

- Ask for feedback in this area from those you lead. Let them know that you want to grow in this quality and need their help. Define for them specific manifestations of how discretion might be demonstrated in leadership, and ask them for their thoughts. Consider making the feedback anonymous or to a third party so that people are free to be honest. Just knowing that their leader is seeking to grow in this area will be inspirational and motivational to all who follow your leadership!

- Are you a verbal processor? Ask those who know you best to help you become more aware of the impressions you leave with others as you dialog with them. Have your team give you feedback on your leadership of team discussions and your involvement in those discussions.

- Read and meditate on Daniel 1:1-17, and note how Daniel demonstrated discretion in relating to the king's request. Note especially how he related to the one in charge of him and his friends as well as his discretion in relating to the king.

- Ask those who know you well and whom you trust to give you honest feedback regarding the way you dress. Ask them specifically if they sense any lack of discretion in your appearance.

- Study the Gospels and note how Jesus demonstrated discretion when interacting with those around Him—both His friends and His enemies. Look for applications to your life and leadership.

- Study the book of Acts and note how Paul demonstrated discretion when interacting with those around him—both his friends and his enemies. Look for applications to your life and leadership.

- Take time to reflect on those with whom you have had conflict in the past twelve months. As you think about those situations, do you recognize a lack of discretion on your part that contributed to the conflict? What does the Lord want you to do about it?

The Competencies of Godly Wisdom

COUNSEL

Here are some practical exercises to help you grow in the area of counsel.

- Read the book of Proverbs and note the number of passages that relate to listening to wisdom and wise counsel and the consequences of this action. Look for applications to your current life situations.

- Reflect on your recent leadership-team discussions. Does the Lord bring to mind any situation where you did not listen to others or give sound counsel? Did you tell others what to do instead of helping them arrive at their own decisions? What is He asking you to do about it?

- Ask those who know you well if they would seek out your counsel in any areas of life. What would those areas be, and why would they want your counsel in them? Perhaps these are areas of strength, and you can begin developing them even more for greater impact.

- If you are currently receiving conflicting or differing advice regarding a situation, ask God to give you wisdom to know which counsel is from Him (or whether both are *not* from Him). Ask Him for insights into His Word that have bearing on this issue.

- Study the books of 1 and 2 Timothy and note how much advice Paul gives Timothy and on what topics.

- Reflect on the sources of counsel—both people and other resources—that are currently available to help you become wise. Should you turn away from some of them or pursue others more at this time?

- Think through and study a biblical topic that you are interested in and would like to coach or counsel another in. After thorough study and reflection, consolidate your thoughts into a concise series of brief ideas and Bible passages that relate to this topic. Expect God to bring someone into your life with whom you can share this. Ask for feedback afterward to better help others in this same area in the future.

- The next time you are in a discussion where several people are sharing their thoughts or opinions, don't talk. Instead, prayerfully reflect on the discussion and wait to see if anyone asks for your opinion or ideas. You'll find that many people will eventually share what you would have, and that when (if) asked, your ideas will be better received and sharper in content.

SOUND JUDGMENT

Here are some practical exercises to help you grow in the area of sound judgment.

- Ask for feedback in this area from those you lead. Let them know that you want to grow in this quality and need their help. Define for them specific manifestations of how exercising sound judgment might be demonstrated in leadership, and ask them for their thoughts. Consider making the feedback anonymous or to a third party so that people are free to be honest. Just knowing that their leader is seeking to grow in this area will be inspirational and motivational to all who follow your leadership!

- Read chapters 1–9 of Proverbs and note the number of passages that relate to pursuing wisdom and outcomes in the life of one who attains it. Look for personal applications from these passages.

- Ask those you supervise if you help them solve their problems or micromanage them. Ask them for suggestions to help you supervise them well.

- Give your leadership team permission to tell you when you make decisions that may lack sound judgment.

- Read a biography of a leader you admire. Note where they exercised sound judgment in their life or leadership. Discuss these observations with your spouse or a friend.

- Reflect on the amount of time you spend in God's Word and prayer. Are you getting enough input from Him to live and lead from an overflow? Are you remaining attached to the Vine of Life (John 15:1-8)? What does He want you to do?

- Study a Bible character who seemed to exercise sound judgment. After thorough study and reflection, consolidate your thoughts into a concise series of brief ideas and Bible passages that relate to this topic. Expect God to bring someone into your life with whom you can share this.

- Reflect on your current lifestyle choices: use of time, standard of living, use of money, pace of life, recreation and exercise, leisure activities and hobbies, and so forth. Do these choices reflect an eternal or temporal value system? What does God want you to do about it?

UNDERSTANDING

Here are some practical exercises to help you grow in the area of understanding.

- Read chapters 1–9 of Proverbs and note the number of passages that relate to pursuing wisdom and outcomes in the life of one who attains it. Make personal applications from your study.

- Ask those you are supervising how you can help them grow in their understanding of themselves or their responsibility. Ask them for suggestions to help you supervise them well.

- Give your leadership team permission to tell you when they sense you are making decisions without adequate understanding.

- Study the ministry of Jesus and note when He conformed to Jewish culture and when He confronted Jewish culture and traditions. Seek to understand why He did different things in different contexts.

- Pursue a new area of knowledge that relates to leadership, seeking to understand how it applies to your current context. Dialogue with either a team member or a peer on how you can integrate what you are learning into your leadership.

- Study the book of Acts and note how Paul sought to apply the principles of contextualized ministry stated in 1 Corinthians 9:19-23. Where did Paul seek to conform to Greek culture and where did he seek to conform to Jewish culture? Where do we see him confronting both?

- Read a biography of a cross-cultural missionary (e.g., William Carey, Amy Carmichael, James O. Fraser, Gladys Aylward, Hudson Taylor), looking for how they integrated wise understanding into their lives and ministries.

POWER

Here are some practical exercises to help you grow in the area of wisely using power.

- Ask for feedback on your use of power from those you lead. Let them know that you want to grow in this quality and need their help. Define for them specific manifestations of how wisely exercising power might be demonstrated in leadership, and ask them for their thoughts. Consider making the feedback anonymous or to a third party so that people are free to be honest. Just knowing that their leader is seeking to grow in this area will be inspirational and motivational to all who follow your leadership!

- Ask those you are supervising if you help them solve their problems or micromanage them. Ask them for suggestions to help you supervise them well.

- Give your leadership team permission to tell you when they see you controlling instead of empowering.

- List some of the challenges or problems you are currently facing in your leadership. Whom can you delegate some responsibility and authority to that they might help you address these issues?

- Study the books of 1 and 2 Kings and 1 and 2 Chronicles, noting the many kings who failed to use their leadership power wisely. What lessons can you draw from their poor examples that will help you to not fall into the same patterns?

- Study the life of David, and note how he exercised power wisely. How can you imitate his example? What can you learn from his failures with Bathsheba (2 Samuel 11:1-27) and with numbering his fighting men (1 Chronicles 21:1-17)?

- Pray over 1 Samuel 10:6 the next time you speak publicly, asking God's Spirit to change you into a different person (His instrument) and empower you and your words, so that lives might be changed through this message.

The Characteristics of Godly Wisdom

Here are some practical exercises to help you grow in these seven characteristics of godly wisdom.

- *Pure*—Give your leadership team or some trusted friends permission to question you about any area of your life that seems to compromise God's truth or commingle the world's beliefs and values with Kingdom beliefs and values.

- *Peace-loving*—Reflect on your relationships. Does the Lord bring anyone to mind that you have an unresolved conflict with? What does He want you to do to initiate resolution?

- *Considerate*—Have you been harsh or abrupt with someone recently? Do you need to seek their forgiveness?

- *Submissive*—Have you thanked your supervisor for their leadership and watchfulness recently? Begin praying for them regularly.

- *Full of mercy and good fruit*—Who is the Lord putting in your life for you to serve in some loving, unselfish act? What does He want you to do about it?

- *Impartial*—Reflect on your recent leadership decisions, both operational and personnel. Have you been impartial in your decision-making? If not, what does He want you to do about it?

- *Sincere*—Give your assistant or a team member permission to challenge you on any work-related expenses you report that they question.

- Read and study the book of Ecclesiastes, looking for applications for your life and leadership.

- Ask someone to mentor you in a specific area of strength. Submit yourself to their example by showing a humble teachability to what they have learned and experienced in this area.

- Ask God to search your heart for any self-serving, self-promoting, or duplicitous behavior. Respond with obedience to whatever He points out.

NOTES

INTRODUCTION

1. D. L. Moody, quoted by Rick Warren, *Rick Warren's Bible Study Methods: Twelve Ways You Can Unlock God's Word* (Grand Rapids, MI: Zondervan, 2006), 16.
2. The Navigators, *Topical Memory System: Hide God's Word in Your Heart* (Colorado Springs, CO: NavPress, 2017).

CHAPTER 2: PRUDENCE

1. Paul J. Achtemeier, ed., *Harper's Bible Dictionary* (San Francisco: Harper & Row, 1985), 954–55.
2. The gallery in Wesley's chapel included a "motif in relief supposedly chosen by Wesley: a dove with an olive branch in its beak encircled by a serpent following its own tail"; Jenny Kingsley, "The House and Chapel of John Wesley," Artistic Miscellany, accessed October 24, 2018, http://artisticmiscellany.com/2016/01/27/the-house-and-chapel-of-john-wesley/.
3. Paraphrase of "Today's problems come from yesterday's 'solutions,'" Peter M. Senge, *The Fifth Discipline: The Art and Practice of the Learning Organization* (New York: Doubleday, 2006), 57.
4. Martin H. Manser et al., *The Complete Topical Guide to the Bible* (Grand Rapids, MI: Baker Books, 2017).

CHAPTER 3: KNOWLEDGE

1. Jeff Schultz, "How Much Data Is Created on the Internet Each Day?," *Micro Focus Blog*, October 10, 2017, https://blog.microfocus.com/how-much-data-is-created-on-the-internet-each-day/.

2. Boban Docevski, "Damascus Blacksmiths Had Made Steel Blades with Carbon Nanotubes Long Before They Were Scientifically Discovered," The Vintage News (website), April 3, 2017, https://www.thevintagenews.com/2017/04/03/damascus -blacksmiths-had-made-steel-blades-with-carbon-nanotubes-long-before-they-were -scientifically-discovered/.

3. "A Very Brief History of Damascus Steel," Clay Smith Guns, accessed October 24, 2018, http://www.claysmithguns.com/knives_history.htm.

4. M. H. Cressey, "Knowledge," in *New Bible Dictionary*, 3rd ed., D. R. W. Wood, ed. (Downers Grove, IL: InterVarsity Press, 1996), 657–58.

5. For more information, see Tom Yeakley, *Growing Kingdom Character: Practical, Intentional Tools for Developing Leaders* (Colorado Springs, CO: NavPress, 2011).

6. Quoted from one of his Daily Hope devotionals: Rick Warren, "God is Never in a Hurry," PastorRick.com, September 3, 2018; https://pastorrick.com/god-is-never -in-a-hurry/.

CHAPTER 4: DISCRETION

1. Interestingly, the temple tax mentioned was not an Old Testament tax but rather one instituted by Zerubbabel during the intertestamental period to help rebuild and maintain the temple after the Jews returned from exile. Jesus willingly paid this tax, adapting himself to a societal rule that was not part of the Old Testament law.

CHAPTER 5: COUNSEL

1. Achtemeier, *Harper's Bible Dictionary*, 190.

CHAPTER 6: SOUND JUDGMENT

1. Francis Brown, S. R. Driver, and Charles A. Briggs, *Enhanced Brown-Driver-Briggs Hebrew and English Lexicon* (Oak Harbor, WA: Logos Research Systems, 2000), 444.

2. L. Goldberg, "923 ישׁה," in *Theological Wordbook of the Old Testament*, ed. R. Laird Harris, Gleason L. Archer Jr., and Bruce K. Waltke (Chicago: Moody Press, 1980), 413.

CHAPTER 7: UNDERSTANDING

1. M. H. Manser, ed., *Dictionary of Bible Themes: The Accessible and Comprehensive Tool for Topical Studies* (London: Martin Manser, 2009), s.v. "8355 understanding," accessed October 21, 2018, via Logos software.

2. Goldberg, "239 בִּין," *Theological Wordbook of the Old Testament*, 103.

3. Paul B. Watney, "Contextualization and Its Biblical Precedents" (PhD diss., Fuller Theological Seminary, 1985), 218.

4. Thom Hopler, *A World of Difference: Following Christ beyond Your Cultural Walls* (Downers Grove, IL: InterVarsity Press, 1981), 65.

5. Jürgen K. Zangenberg, "The Samaritans," Bible Odyssey, accessed October 25, 2018, https://www.bibleodyssey.org/en/people/related-articles/samaritans.

6. Adapted from my 2013 blog post: Tom Yeakley, "The 'Confrontational' Model of Jesus," *Developing Kingdom Leaders* (blog), November 25, 2013, https:// developingkingdomleaders.com/2013/11/.

7. Merrill F. Unger, *Unger's Bible Dictionary*, 3rd ed. (Chicago: Moody Press, 1985), 362.

8. Alfred Edersheim, *The Life and Times of Jesus the Messiah*, book IV, chap. III (McLean, VA: MacDonald Publishing, 1980), 111.

CHAPTER 8: POWER

1. See William R. Moody, *The Life of Dwight L. Moody* (Murfreesboro, TN: Sword of the Lord, 1900) and Dwight Lyman Moody, *Secret Power, or The Success in Christian Life and Christian Work* (New York: Revell, 1881).

CONCLUSION: THE CHARACTERISTICS OF GODLY WISDOM

1. Adapted from *Beginning the Walk: 18 Sessions on Jesus the Way, the Truth, and the Life* (Colorado Springs: NavPress, 2018), 177.

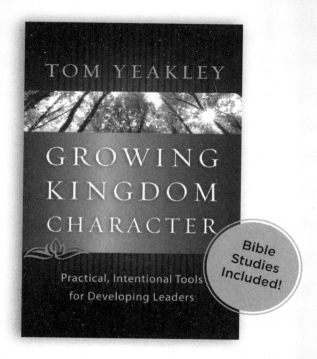

THE NAVIGATORS® STORY

THANK YOU for picking up this NavPress book! I hope it has been a blessing to you.

NavPress is a ministry of The Navigators. The Navigators began in the 1930s, when a young California lumberyard worker named Dawson Trotman was impacted by basic discipleship principles and felt called to teach those principles to others. He saw this mission as an echo of 2 Timothy 2:2: "And the things you have heard me say in the presence of many witnesses entrust to reliable people who will also be qualified to teach others" (NIV).

In 1933, Trotman and his friends began discipling members of the US Navy. By the end of World War II, thousands of men on ships and bases around the world were learning the principles of spiritual multiplication by the intentional, person-to-person teaching of God's Word.

After World War II, The Navigators expanded its relational ministry to include college campuses; local churches; the Glen Eyrie Conference Center and Eagle Lake Camps in Colorado Springs, Colorado; and neighborhood and citywide initiatives across the country and around the world.

Today, with more than 2,600 US staff members—and local ministries in more than 100 countries—The Navigators continues the transformational process of making disciples who make more disciples, advancing the Kingdom of God in a world that desperately needs the hope and salvation of Jesus Christ and the encouragement to grow deeper in relationship with Him.

NAVPRESS was created in 1975 to advance the calling of The Navigators by bringing biblically rooted and culturally relevant products to people who want to know and love Christ more deeply. In January 2014, NavPress entered an alliance with Tyndale House Publishers to strengthen and better position our rich content for the future. Through *THE MESSAGE* Bible and other resources, NavPress seeks to bring positive spiritual movement to people's lives.

If you're interested in learning more or becoming involved with The Navigators, go to www.navigators.org. For more discipleship content from The Navigators and NavPress authors, visit www.thedisciplemaker.org. May God bless you in your walk with Him!

Sincerely,

DON PAPE
VP/PUBLISHER, NAVPRESS

NavPress
www.navpress.com

CP1308